PET SITTING FOR PROFIT

PET SITTING FOR PROFIT
3rd Edition

PATTI J. MORAN

Illustrations by Michelle Boles

0 8 5 8 6 6

Howell Book House
Published by Wiley Publishing, Inc., Hoboken, New Jersey

For general information on our other products and services or to obtain technical support please contact our Customer Care Department within the U.S. at (800) 762-2974, outside the U.S. at (317) 572-3993 or fax (317) 572-4002.

Wiley also publishes its books in a variety of electronic formats. Some content that appears in print may not be available in electronic books. For more information about Wiley products, please visit our web site at www.wiley.com.

Library of Congress Cataloging-in-Publication Data:
Moran, Patti J.
  Pet sitting for profit / Patti J. Moran ; illustrations by Michelle Boles.-- 3rd ed.
     p. cm.
  Includes index.
  ISBN-13: 978-0-7645-9635-3 (cloth)
  ISBN-10: 0-7645-9635-7 (cloth)
  1. Pet sitting--Handbooks, manuals, etc. 2. New business enterprises--Handbooks, manuals, etc.
I. Title.
  SF414.34.M67 2006
  636.088'7--dc22   2005037196

Printed in the United States of America

10 9 8 7 6 5 4 3 2 1

Third Edition

Book design by LeAndra Hosier
Cover design by José Almaguer
Cover photography by Robin K. Underhill of Ruby's Photography
Book production by Wiley Publishing, Inc. Composition Services

For all the people who said "You're gonna do what?" and for the thousands of professional pet sitters who have helped me to establish pet sitting as a respected, credible, and rewarding career.

Contents

Preface

Many readers have been curious about my background, how I came up with the idea of pet sitting, and how I came to write a book about the subject. Others have asked if I intentionally set out to create an industry. So, for those who are interested in such things, I offer the following.

It all started in 1983 when I was laid off from my job. Actually, people in management positions are terminated (as opposed to laid off) when companies downsize. Whatever you want to call it, I found myself unemployed. If anyone had told me then that losing my job was a blessing in disguise, I wouldn't have believed it. I had been hired by a large manufacturing company one week after graduating from college. I spent seven years there in employee relations, working my way up from a clerical position to management. My position was stress-filled due to the workload and company politics. The salary and benefits, however, were generous, and somehow I resigned myself to the fact that it was easier to stay than to leave. When the company experienced a severe downturn in business, almost half the employees, including me, found themselves without a job.

Because I needed the income, I started exploring my job options. The idea of having my own business had always appealed to me, and at that point it was more attractive than ever. The thought of not having to answer to anyone else or depend upon anyone else for job security encouraged me to seriously consider starting my own business. My biggest question was what kind of business to start.

As I slowly researched various ideas, I also took time out for myself. I planted a garden. I took classes. I mowed the grass on cool weekday mornings. I noticed the angle of the sun at various hours of the day. I shopped at times when there was hardly anyone in the stores. These activities were all luxuries to me after seven years in the corporate rat race, years when time was limited and dictated by the demands of my job. I rapidly became spoiled by my flexible schedule, and the idea of an eight-to-five office job actually grew abhorrent.

What could I do that would provide adequate income and allow me time to enjoy this newfound and treasured lifestyle?

The answer came when a good friend who'd recently moved to another city visited for a weekend. Knowing how crazy she was about her dog, I asked what type of arrangements she had made for her pet's care during her absence. She told me she had hired a pet sitter to come to her house twice a day. Little did I know then that this innocent question and her answer would change my life as I knew it . . . but it was then and there that the light bulb went on in my head. I was immediately intrigued!

Having three dogs and a cat of my own at the time, I was all too familiar with the problems a pet owner faces when traveling. I knew firsthand that a pet-sitting service would be a needed and welcome option in my community. Furthermore, pet sitting could be done in just a few hours in the morning and the late afternoon, so I'd have some flexibility and extra hours in my day for other activities. It wouldn't require a costly inventory and I certainly wouldn't need an expensive wardrobe. I also didn't see any need for renting office space initially; pet sitting seemed to me to be an ideal choice for a home-based business. And because I loved animals, pet sitting would enable me to get paid for doing something I enjoyed. It quickly became apparent to me that a pet-sitting business had many advantages and incorporated all the things I was looking for in a new career. Although it was scary to consider the risk I'd be taking in opening an unheard-of business in our town, I felt I should at least give it a try.

As I made preparations to open my pet-sitting service, there were times when I thought I might be crazy. First, although there was a lot of information available about how to start a small business, I couldn't find any information that specifically addressed pet sitting. Second, I was often not taken seriously when I told people what I was attempting to do. Some of my friends just couldn't believe I planned to "baby-sit for pets and clean litter boxes for a living." And, as I searched for business insurance coverage, many doors were shut in my face.

But, as the saying goes, where there's a will, there's a way. In late 1983, my pet-sitting service opened for business. Since that time, this relatively new and innovative business has provided me with a very rewarding, interesting, and profitable career.

I was originally prompted to write this book for a couple of reasons. As people in other parts of the country heard about my business, I began receiving requests for help and information from budding entrepreneurs who wanted to start such a business in their own area. Because there was nothing available in writing to help me when I first started pet sitting, I knew firsthand the need for such guidance. I also wrote the book (and initially published it myself) because I believed that pet sitting is a viable profession. It provides a valuable service for pets and their owners and an enjoyable and profitable way for pet lovers to earn a livelihood.

In writing the book to help others get started more easily, did I set out to create an industry? No. One step just naturally led to another—with several steps being suggested by readers and colleagues along the way. This book and the information it contains launched others into the career.

With the proliferation came the request for products and items that would be useful to professional pet sitters (and thus launched my products company, Patti Moran's), and the need for an organization to unite pet sitters soon followed. While I joke and say it's good that I didn't know all the work I was getting into (ignorance is bliss!) with my passion for pet sitting, I am very grateful for the accolades afforded my efforts. I have worked very hard to advance the profession of pet sitting and, being only human, find it's nice and gratifying to have my endeavors recognized and appreciated.

Do I still own and operate a pet-sitting business? No. It was with some sadness—and a lot of pride—that I sold my ten-year-old service in November 1993. I had not done any hands-on pet sitting (the fun part of the business!) in almost seven years, because managing the business had become almost a full-time job. Trying to run it, along with a pet-sitting association and a pet-sitting products company, had become a bit much. So when an offer came along that I couldn't refuse, I did sell my local service so I could concentrate my time and energies toward growing, improving, and supporting professional pet sitting on a larger scale.

To an extent, selling my business was like letting go of a child. It was something I had lovingly and carefully nurtured and built. At the same time, it was exhilarating to build a business that had value and was salable! And with selling my business, a new milestone in pet sitting was reached. No longer was pet sitting a business to be laughed at; instead it had become an established, profitable business to buy!

I'm happy to say that my former business is still in operation twenty-some years later. But due to the strong demand for pet sitters and the ever-increasing popularity of our services, it's no longer the only pet-sitting business in town!

—Patti Moran

Acknowledgments

One of the best things about pet sitting is that you meet the nicest people. And after twenty-some years in this field, there are so many people near and dear to me in some way that I almost hesitate to make acknowledgments for fear of leaving someone out. I could write a book, or at least a long chapter, simply recalling memories with certain folks or just thanking dedicated pet sitters who have touched my life during my pet-sitting career. But since space is short, I can only acknowledge a few who have shared in this adventure and, by having been a part of it, have made the uphill climb easier, possible, or just more fun.

My love and thanks to Dotty and to the other staff I've been blessed to work with at Pet Sitters International who love what we do and who have contributed greatly in making PSI the organization it is today: Kay C., Ellen, Michelle, and Amy. To longtime pet sitters and friends Debbie H., Cynthia, and Alice, who have been supporters and friends from the beginning. To my friend Debbie L., who turned the light bulb on for me, and to her sister, Barbara, for doing this with me when most of the world looked askance. To visionaries like Bud, who recognized early on the important and influential role professional pet sitters would have in the pet care arena. To the pet sitters or "critter sitters" who worked for me, Pam, Annabelle, Malinda, Kay L., and Eleanor, and helped to build a reputation of excellence in pet sitting way back then. And to my three angels, Lucy, Lonnie, and Ennis, who I think would be proud. And to Mike—who I know is.

Introduction

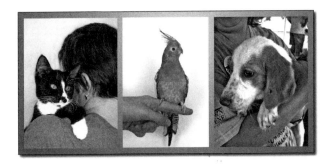

No one knows what he can do till he tries.

—*Publilius Syrus, Maxim 786*

Whatever you think you can do, or dream you can do, begin it. Boldness has genius, magic, and power in it.

—*Goethe*

If at once you have begun, never leave it till it's done. Be it big or be it small, do it well or not at all.

—*My mother*

At least I won't be sitting in a rocker on the porch of a nursing home saying, "You know, I wish I'd started that business. . . ."

—*Anyone*

There's never been a better time to become a professional pet sitter. Thanks to the love affair we're having with our pets, Americans have doubled what we spend on pets since 1994, from $17 billion annually then to $34.4 billion in 2004, according to the American Pet Products Manufacturers Association (APPMA). In 2005, annual pet expenditures are expected to reach $36 billion as the "pets as family" concept expands nationwide.

Today's pet owner wants for their pet what they'd like for themselves or for their children. From technological and educational toys to vehicle restraints to designer clothing, pet moms and dads want only the best for their furry, feathered, or finny babies.

Is it any wonder that we're living in such a pet-crazed society? Pets add so much to our lives—companionship, unconditional love, purpose, security, and just plain fun. Studies now substantiate that pets help to lower blood pressure, reduce stress, fight depression, and prevent heart disease. The fact that pets are now thought of as true family members has been evidenced in findings from the American Animal Hospital Association's 2004 Pet Owner Survey:

- 94 percent of pet owners think their pet has humanlike personality traits, such as being emotional, or seems outgoing, inquisitive, or stubborn.

- 94 percent take their pets for regular veterinary checkups to ensure their pet's quality of life.

- 93 percent are likely to risk their own life for their pet, while 64 percent of owners would expect their pet to come to their rescue if they were in distress.

- 82 percent think of their pet more than once while they are away from him or her during the day.

- 70 percent break "household rules" (letting the pet on the bed, giving an extra treat) when their spouse or significant other is away.

- 55 percent have an emergency preparedness plan in case of natural disasters such as fire, flood, or earthquake that includes their pet.

- 53 percent are spending more on their pets now than they did three years ago.

From the 2003 survey:

- 39 percent gave their pet a human name.

- 47 percent said their pet most often sleeps on their bed.

- 62 percent celebrate or recognize their pet's birthday.

And from 2002:

- 70 percent said they sign their pet's name on greeting cards.

- 58 percent said their pet is included in family or holiday portraits.

- 39 percent said they have more photos of their pet than of their spouse or significant other.

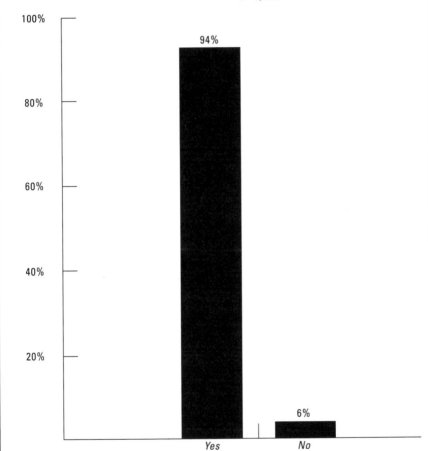

Does Your Pet Have Human-Like Personality Traits?

n=1,221

Source: American Animal Hospital Association 2004 National Pet Owner Survey

These polls of pet owners in the United States and Canada indicate that pets are receiving preferential treatment and pampering like never before. People have gone to the dogs, cats, birds, fish, rabbits, reptiles, and more. So have professional pet sitters.

When I reflect on the years since 1983, the year I started my pet-sitting business, it's almost overwhelming to consider the social changes in *admitted* attitudes toward pets and the coincidental growth in pet sitting.

One of the reasons becoming a pet sitter initially appealed to me was simply the fact that my husband and I had three dogs who were like children to us. The option of having a mature, responsible adult come to our home to care for them when we needed to travel just seemed to be the kinder, gentler way. At least if we couldn't be with them, they would have all the other comforts of their home. Even though this was some twenty years ago, I thought that if I felt this way about my pets, then surely there were people out there who doted on their pets the way I did!

Little did I know it was like opening a dam. I laughingly say that the advent of professional pet sitters allowed eccentric pet owners to come out of the closet. It took building trust and a rapport with clients, but once they knew my pet sitters and I wanted to follow their pet's routine as closely as possible, out came the requests. Can you scramble eggs with cheese for them each morning? Will you fluff his bed sheets in the dryer every day? Will you let her listen to my voice on the answering machine during each visit? It was just as I suspected: I wasn't the only one out there who was totally bonkers over my pet!

Through my years in this field, I've seen a big change in social attitudes. At first people were hesitant to admit their deep love for their pets—and hesitant to use a pet sitter. But as it became more accepted to acknowledge these feelings, we've sort of gone 180 degrees. Now the sky is the limit for our pets and good pet sitters are in demand. The trend is not expected to change, either, because spending on pets by adults ages 55 to 64 is expected to grow the fastest of all age groups in the next few years, and this is a huge age group because it comprises the aging Baby Boomers. Following are the Gen-Xers and the Millenniums (the labeled generations after) who have grown up with pets being more like family members and who are likely to sustain the pampered-pet attitude.

While it's true that some people and some communities still are not familiar with the at-home pet care services provided by professional pet sitters, the industry has truly come a long way. It is a changed (and much more receptive) world for pet sitting, much different from what I experienced back in 1983! Today's pet sitter does not have to endure the laughs from skeptics who ask in disbelief, "You do what?" (Well, there probably will always be a few you'll have to grin and bear . . .) Nor does today's pet sitter have to spend hours looking for good business liability coverage—a tailor-made policy exists for our burgeoning industry.

No longer is trial and error a mandatory part of the learning process for today's pet-sitting professional. Tried and true procedures, methods, and tips are readily available in publications such as this, along with other numerous resources, such as professional organizations, web sites, and products that are specifically made for pet sitters.

Although today's pet sitter will make some mistakes (no matter how many times I advise you always to test a client's house key, you will still find yourself locked out of a house before you make it a practice to do so), there aren't really a whole lot of excuses available if you've done your homework. If you're seriously considering professional pet sitting as a career, the best homework assignment I can give you is to read this book. In it, I've compiled the best—and the worst—of my experiences in pet sitting. I include a lot of hard-won lessons and expertise—not only from me, but from many of my colleagues as well.

Having the opportunity to write this book, as well as to found two pet-sitting associations (national and international), has put me in direct contact with many other professionals in the field. We all have learned and grown professionally from this contact and communication. Many of us have become good friends in the process. Since selling my pet-sitting business in 1993 to devote more time to promoting professional pet sitting, much of my pet sitting has been done vicariously—through the eyes, ears, and experiences of colleagues who actively pet sit. My initial requests from eccentric pet owners who wanted a special meal prepared or a game played with their pet now seem tame compared to the stories related to me by colleagues! Never was I asked to actually drive a dog around the block (talk about pampered) or sing show tunes to a parrot or care for a pet lobster originally intended as an edible gift. . . . But, thanks to my colleagues, pet sitting still remains fascinating and fun even from my desk, and I continue to learn, grow, and enjoy this adventure.

In all my years in pet sitting, something that has become increasingly clear is that there is no one way to run a pet-sitting service. Because each pet, customer, home, and assignment is different, there is no "one size fits all" when it comes to pet sitting. You would be wise to read and learn as much as possible about this career so that you can make the right choices in your own pet-sitting business.

Due to the ever-changing, ever-growing nature of pet sitting, I'm convinced that no one can know it all or have all the answers. Although some flatter me by saying I'm the wise old sage of the business, I'll be the first to tell you that I don't begin to know it all! What I do know is that people attracted to this career seem to be the nicest people and care about being their professional best. And by sharing experiences, we can continue to learn and improve and grow together.

A friend recently asked why I was spending so much time revising and expanding this book when the previous editions have sold so well. Several reasons immediately came to mind.

First, in anything I do, I like to do it well (thanks in large part to my dear late mother, who is quoted at the beginning of this introduction). This philosophy was evident in the first editions of *Pet Sitting for Profit*, and I believe my thoroughness is what has earned my book its reputation as the "bible of pet sitting." With such high praise from thousands of readers, I unknowingly created equally high expectations for subsequent editions!

Second, as I previously mentioned, the pet-sitting industry continues to evolve. In each book revision, I have attempted to address the trends that were taking place within the industry and the relevant issues. For example, the critical need for good (but often difficult to obtain) business liability insurance was stressed in earlier editions. Thanks to the proliferation of pet sitters in recent years, this need has been recognized by the insurance industry and an excellent policy has been made available. However, with the increase in pet-sitting services, subsequent editions stressed the need to protect the name of your business. When there were only a handful of pet sitters, name recognition and protection weren't given a second thought. In earlier editions, I stressed the importance of giving careful consideration to this facet of starting and running a business. Similarly, in this edition I will attempt to keep you on the cutting edge of what is happening in professional pet sitting.

A third motivation has come from you, the reader. Many of you have written to ask me questions, solicit advice, or share your own experiences in starting and operating your pet-sitting businesses. Although I have not been able to reply personally in all cases, I have read and appreciated your communications. And through them, I've become aware of mutual concerns and areas that need more attention in revised editions of *Pet Sitting for Profit*. I thank you for letting me know how I can improve this book and better help the pet sitters of tomorrow. I sincerely hope this new edition meets the high standards you've come to expect from me.

Being at the forefront of this industry, I have seen it grow from only a handful of us back in 1983 to an estimated 7,500 companies in the United States today. Even with this phenomenal growth, I firmly believe that this field is still in its infancy. I see parallels between pet sitting and pizza—if you'll indulge me for just a minute.

I remember, as a kid growing up in the 1960s, how pizza—while certainly not a new dish in food history—experienced what can be described as a food revolution. In our home, it was something different for dinner and really quite a treat. However, the only way to have a pizza back then was to make it from scratch or from a mix. Then came the 1970s, when pizzerias and pizza restaurant chains opened up all across the country. The love affair with pizza continued into the 1980s, with home deliveries of pizza, numerous pizza chains, and all sorts of frozen varieties and ready-made crusts widely available in stores. Today pizza is still big business; there's a pizza shop (or two!) in every community. Pizza has become a household staple.

Professional pet sitting has gone through a similar evolution. It was a fairly new concept in the 1980s, but as the pet-owning consumer's awareness has grown about the advantages of in-home pet care, so has the demand. Although there isn't a pet sitter on every block in America yet, pet sitters are starting to specialize in cat care or bird care or horse care. The progress has come with the public's perception and acceptance—and a warm one at that—of the use of professional pet sitters. In the twenty-first century, calling a pet sitter is as natural as ordering a pizza.

There are a couple of reasons I think pet sitting offers tremendous career opportunities and is still nowhere near the size of the industry it will become. One is that it lends itself beautifully to being a small, home-based business. I've heard from countless stay-at-home moms (and a few dads!) who were delighted to learn that professional pet sitting has become a credible occupation. "I was doing this anyway for everyone in the neighborhood," they've told me. Now they're turning these time-consuming neighborhood favors into small, income-producing business ventures. With changes in our Social Security laws that may delay when retirement benefits can be drawn, more senior adults may need additional income, and professional pet sitting offers a fun and gratifying way to earn it.

One of the great things about pet sitting is that it can be done on a small scale in a neighborhood subdivision or condominium complex—or it can be done on a large scale with a staff of pet sitters covering a wide city/county area. One thing is for sure: Pets are everywhere; in subdivisions, at apartment complexes, on rural farms—and they all need conscientious daily care.

How many pets are there? According to the 2004 National Pet Owners Survey conducted by the APPMA, there are 100 million more pets than people in the United States!

The survey found 63 percent of U.S. households own a pet—that's 64.2 million pet-owning U.S. households. Based on the 2000 U.S. Census, 36 percent of American households have children. This means almost twice as many households have pets than have children (and treat them like children!) and 45 percent of all households own more than one pet.

The table below shows the breakdown of pet ownership in the United States:

	2004	2005
Cats	77.7 million	90.5 million
Dogs	65 million	73.9 million
Birds	17.3 million	16.6 million
Reptiles	9 million	11 million
Small mammals	16.8 million	18.2 million
Saltwater fish	7 million	9.6 million
Freshwater fish	185 million	139 million

Source: American Pet Products Manufacturers Association

Based on member surveys conducted by Pet Sitters International, it's estimated that professional pet sitters serve an estimated one million clients annually. This means there are 63.2 million pet-owning households out there who still need a pet sitter. While our industry has made terrific strides in growth and public awareness, we have less than 1 percent of the pet-owning market's business. This is the second reason I believe pet sitting has tremendous career potential: There is a lot more business out there to be garnered by existing—and new—pet sitters. Apparently, the U.S. Bureau of Labor Statistics agrees; according to a May 1, 2002, article in *American Demographics*, they report that "the number of 'animal caretakers' is expected to grow much faster than average—22 percent between 2000 and 2010—as more consumers seek out professional care for their pets."

Before you get all dizzy from dollar signs in your eyes, let me stress that there is a lot more to pet sitting than meets the eye. It's not, as some would think, a fast way to make a buck. Calling yourself a pet sitter is not enough to be successful in today's business world. Loving animals is not even enough to ensure your success in pet sitting. All too often I've heard of pet sitters who get into this business thinking their love and enjoyment of animals will sustain them. Then, three or four months down the road, they're out of business. These fly-by-nights reflect poorly upon the industry. Therefore, I urge you, as a prospective entrepreneur, to give this promising and unique venture your careful consideration.

As I mentioned at the outset, there's no better time to be a pet sitter. The market is there—the educational curve has taken place, making "pet sitter" a household term—and pet-sitting pioneers have come before you, overcoming obstacles to success. There is so much knowledge available to today's pet sitter that there's almost no excuse for failure. You don't have to reinvent the wheel; all you have to do is make the commitment to follow in the footsteps of those who have come before you, who have set the standard for excellence in pet sitting.

Consider all the angles and the necessary ingredients to running a successful pet-sitting service—above all keeping in mind that it is a business. Careful forethought will ensure that your journey into pet sitting will be a successful and satisfying venture. And now, read on.

Chapter 1

The Concept of Pet Sitting

It was a proud moment in July 1997 when Random House released a revised edition of their dictionary that contained the phrase *pet sitter*. You can imagine my surprise in learning that after thirteen years of being in this career, I found it was not even mentioned in any of the English dictionaries! No wonder people hadn't been familiar with pet sitters; officially, we didn't exist!

Thanks to a letter-writing campaign conducted by Pet Sitters International, that changed when Random House added and defined pet sitter:

Pet sitter—one who cares for the pets of another, usually in the pet's home environment.

The key words in this definition are "in the pet's home environment." To me, it is this unique concept that has played a major role in the popularity of our services. We go to the pet—allowing him to stay in his comfortable and secure surroundings. I know that some professed pet sitters have included in their range of services placing the pet in the home of another caretaker or even bringing the pet into the sitter's own home. To me, this is not pet sitting in its truest sense. Midday dog walking does qualify as pet sitting, though, because the dog walker is actually going to the pet's home to give him a daily dose of exercise and TLC. I realize that some pets do fine as visitors in another household; however, this arrangement is closer to boarding than to pet sitting.

Although the concept of pet sitting is much more widely known now than it was in the 1980s when I was starting out, I constantly hear from people who have just "discovered" the wonderful world of at-home pet care. In some instances, these calls are from pet owners who want to find a good pet sitter. Others are from intrigued "wannabe" pet sitters. This tells me that even though pet sitting has come a long way, we still have much to do in the way of educating the general public. The United States is a huge country with many animal lovers who may not have heard of our relatively young industry, and thus may never have considered pet sitting as a profitable business venture.

WHAT MAKES PET SITTING A GREAT CAREER

Pet sitting has much to offer as a career. Whether you have just learned of this industry or have been aware of it for some time, I urge you to consider the potential a pet-sitting business can hold—potential for self-employment, for providing a needed community service, for creating the lifestyle you've always dreamed of, and for significant profits.

To start off, you'll be part of the service industry, which is expected to be a powerful economic force in the future. People today need services of all sorts. According to the United States Department of Labor, service-providing industries are expected to account for approximately 20.8 million of the 21.6 million new wage and salary jobs generated over the period from 2002 to 2012.

These figures are very encouraging to anyone thinking of starting a pet-sitting service. With your own pet-sitting business, you'll join the fast track of the new, service-oriented American economy.

If you're a female contemplating getting into pet sitting, you'll be further encouraged to know that the National Foundation for Women Business Owners reports there are now 7.95 million companies owned by women, up from 4.48 million in 1987. This 78 percent growth dwarfs the 47 percent growth for all firms in the United States.

The 2004 membership of Pet Sitters International (PSI), an educational organization for professional pet sitters, was 88 percent female. Although more and more men are getting into this business, pet sitting has been a female-dominated industry to date. Perhaps it naturally attracts women because of the nurturing involved in caring for animals (nurturing has traditionally been associated with women). Whatever the reason, I'm proud that pet sitting has provided a way for many women to enjoy the rewards, personally and professionally, of entrepreneurship. And I am glad to see many men recognizing that pet sitting is a viable and profitable business venture!

Why the Service Economy Is Growing

The following trends in today's society have made service businesses—and pet sitting—fast-growing industries:

● Two-income families have become the norm, making services both needed by and affordable to these families. Travel for pleasure is also more affordable, which increases the likelihood that pet care will be needed during such absences from home.

• Young professionals delay marriage and/or children; many more are owning pets and taking better care of them than ever before.

• The same is true of "empty nesters," who are getting pets and treating them as surrogate children.

In other words, the yuppies of the 1980s have been replaced in the '90s by "dinks" (dual income, no kids) and "dips" (dual income, pets). The "dips" comprise a profitable market for pet sitters!

Another trend in American society is the move toward self-employment, often in a home-based setting. More and more of us are discovering that our jobs rule our lives, and contrary to generations past, we're finding in today's world that there is no such thing as job security. Self-employment enables you to take control of your life, your career, your schedule, and your income. As a pet sitter, you are your own boss. You decide when you work, where you work, what you charge, and for whom you work. There is no one looking over your shoulder and no time clock to punch.

Perhaps due to the downsizing in corporate America, we have become a transient society. People come and go, often not staying in one place long enough to get to know their neighbors. And even if you do know your neighbors, that doesn't mean you want them in your home when you're away or that you feel comfortable requesting pet-care services from them.

Another trend in today's society that has given rise to service industries is that we're a busy society! Geez, how did we get so busy? Never have we had so many conveniences to make life easier, yet it seems we never have enough time to get it all done. Enter house cleaners, lawn services, car detailers, and, yes, pet sitters. (Oh, and let's not forget those pizza delivery people!) Convenience has become the name of the game.

A negative trend that has enhanced the popularity of at-home pet care is the prevalence of property crimes. We see and hear about crime almost every day through the media. Unfortunately, no one and no community is immune from it, and there is a great deal of public concern about crime. People love the fact that by using a professional pet sitter, their home is being checked at the same time that their pets are being cared for. While making pet-care visits, pet sitters provide a measure of crime deterrence because they make the home appear inhabited. This feature, in itself, is a real selling point for our service.

Last, but certainly not least, is the trend in America to anthropomorphize our pets. And here, for a definition, we can turn once again to the dictionary: Anthropomorphism is defined as "the attributing of human shape or characteristics to a god, animal, or inanimate thing." This tendency has elevated the

pet to a full-fledged family member, a surrogate child—the all-important com-
panion who has needs, feelings, thoughts, and personality traits. We talk to our
pets, pamper them, and want only the best for our "babies." The best includes
a pet sitter!

So How Many Pets Did You Say Are Out There?

According to the 2005/2006 American Pet Products Manufacturers
Association (APPMA) National Pet Owner Survey, 63 percent of all U.S.
households own a pet (that's more than 69 million households), up from 56
percent in 1988, when APPMA began doing its survey. The pet population
breaks down as follows:

- Cats: 90.5 million in 37.7 million households

- Dogs: 73.9 million in 43.5 million households

- Freshwater fish: 139 million in 13.9 million households

- Saltwater fish: 9.6 million in 0.8 million households

- Birds: 16.6 million in 6.4 million households

- Small mammals: 18.2 million in 5.7 million households (that includes
rabbits, hamsters, guinea pigs, mice, rats, gerbils, potbellied pigs, and chinchillas)

- Reptiles: 11 million in 4.4 million households (that includes turtles,
tortoises, iguanas, snakes, lizards, frogs, and toads)

Figures were not available from this survey for the number of ferrets or her-
mit crabs kept as pets; however, these animals are found in many pet-owning
households. Livestock figures also were not available, although at-home care of
horses, cows, goats, pigs, sheep, and even ducks and chickens can be an important and profitable business for professional pet sitters.

ALTERNATIVES TO PET SITTING

Let's discuss the traditional choices a pet owner has had in the past and why
personalized home pet care has become such a popular alternative.

When faced with travel, a pet owner usually has called upon a kennel or
veterinarian to board his or her pet. Although some pets do very well in a kennel environment and look forward to it as "camp," many other pets find a

strange environment filled with unfamiliar animals to be an upsetting experience. Many pet owners have told me they have had a vacation spoiled by the memory of those sad and confused eyes they left behind. Some said they even had to tranquilize their pets to transport them to boarding facilities. Older pets, especially, are traumatized by a change in environment.

By calling on the services of a pet sitter, the owner can leave the pet in his own secure, familiar space. Pets are creatures of habit, just as people are; by staying in their own home they are able to follow their normal eating, medication, and exercise routines. Such familiarity contributes to the happiness and health of the pet. Plus, it eliminates the pet owners' need to worry about the welfare of their pet(s).

When using a pet sitter, the owner is not inconvenienced by having to transport their pet to the vet or kennel, nor is there the trauma of traveling for the pet. An additional benefit of staying at home is that the likelihood of exposure to illnesses is greatly reduced for the pet. Perhaps most important, the pet receives loving, individual attention from his or her personal sitter.

Another option pet owners have is to call upon a friend or neighborhood kid to care for their pets when they are away. In today's highly mobile society, many people don't know their neighbors well enough to feel comfortable making this request or just don't want to impose on a friend. What if the neighborhood kid brings in half the neighborhood with him? What if the pet becomes ill or something in the house gets broken? Such circumstances could certainly strain or ruin a friendship.

There is security in calling a professionally operated pet-sitting service that employs sitters who are accustomed to transporting an ill pet to the vet and who also are insured for breakage in a customer's home. A professional pet-sitting service has reliable, responsible, mature, trustworthy individuals who enjoy the business of caring for pets. Pet sitters can be counted on to treat each pet and home as if it were their own.

There are additional benefits to the pet owner. A pet sitter keeps an eye on each home by doing such things as bringing in the mail and newspapers, turning lights on and off, opening and closing curtains or blinds, and watering houseplants. These small services give a home a "lived-in" look while the owner is away. Such crime-deterring measures result in additional peace of mind for the absent homeowner. It is a pleasure for returning homeowners to find healthy and happy pets awaiting their arrival—and their home just as they left it.

A pet sitter is also only a phone call away. Who hasn't left on vacation and thirty miles away from home wondered, "Did I turn off the coffee pot (or iron or oven)?" A phone call to the pet sitter can result in an extra visit to the home that will alleviate this nagging worry!

Expense may be the only negative for a pet owner who engages the services of a pet sitter. A pet sitter is usually a bit more expensive than a kennel (unless it's a multiple-pet household—then using a pet sitter is usually less expensive than a kennel) or a neighbor. But the number of repeat clients I have had and the feedback I got from them attests to the fact that most pet owners think the convenience and advantages offered by a pet sitter are well worth a little extra expense.

THE ADVANTAGES OF OPERATING A PET-SITTING SERVICE

It is true that there is an exhilarating independence and pride that comes from being your own boss. An added bonus is that becoming a business owner will give you an increased sense of self-worth and confidence in your abilities. I've had letters from many stay-at-home mothers who found that their pet-sitting services helped them rebuild their work skills and confidence levels while contributing to the family income. I've heard from retirees who said their pet-sitting service enabled them to remain active and to feel like contributing members of society. The self-satisfaction you'll derive is only one of the many benefits you'll experience as the owner of your own pet-sitting service. Although you may work longer hours, work usually becomes more enjoyable when you're working for yourself.

Being a pet sitter gives you flexibility with your daily routine. You'll no longer be bound by a rigid nine-to-five work schedule. Because most pet-sitting visits are made during the early morning or early evening hours, you'll have the largest part of the day free to pursue other interests or even to work another job. The flexible working hours make pet sitting an ideal part-time business or second income for many people, because pet-sitting responsibilities can be adapted to most schedules. And of course, it can be operated as a full-time business in many cities.

Another important thing that pet sitting has going for it is that work becomes fun! Many sitters have told me that pet sitting is so enjoyable that they almost don't feel like they're working. Each pet, home, and customer is different, adding variety and interest to the job.

Pets and their owners are so appreciative of your efforts, and the pets readily let you know it. Perhaps you have worked for that boss or supervisor whose praise, compliments, or positive "strokes" were few and far between—not so with pet sitting. That wagging tail or contented purring lets you know someone is glad you're there. And pets don't care what you're wearing or how you look. It's a wonderful feeling to wake up on a rainy morning, throw on jeans and a sweatshirt, and head out the door to destinations where you'll be eagerly and warmly greeted.

You'll also take pride in knowing you're providing such a valuable service to your community. Pet owners have had few choices in the past. Traditionally, they could either leave their pets in unfamiliar environments, impose upon a friend or neighbor, or stay home. By opening a pet-sitting service, you're providing a preferred alternative for pet owners, thus enabling them to travel with the assurance that their pets and home are in good hands.

Becoming a pet sitter will provide income, too. Whether you sit independently or employ a staff of sitters, there is money to be made by providing this valuable service to your community.

THE NEED IS EVERYWHERE

One of the most positive factors to consider when evaluating pet sitting as a business is that virtually every community, urban and rural, really needs this service. Where there are people, there are pets. Recent research has confirmed the therapeutic effect pets have on people. Pets help reduce blood pressure, provide purpose, and combat loneliness. And with crime on the rise in many areas, many dogs are finding homes because of the crime-deterrence they provide. Given these incentives for having a pet, the shrinking size of the American family, and the increasing numbers of older people and unmarried adults living alone, it is safe to assume that pet ownership will continue to grow.

To determine if there is a need for a pet-sitting service in your area, check the local Yellow Pages for listings or call veterinarians, groomers, and pet supply stores to see if any such business exists in your community. If you live in a rural area, remember that farmers and livestock owners often have a difficult time leaving home, so your service could be a real godsend. If there is already a service operating and you don't live in a sparsely populated area, there's probably room for more than one pet-sitting business.

HOW MUCH CAN YOU EARN?

Although pet sitting is a terrific business idea, it takes more than a good idea to make a business a success. I'm often asked by readers, "How much can I expect to make?" This is one question I can't answer. I don't know the reader's capabilities, desires, and level of commitment.

The amount of income you can expect to make will depend on several variables. The location of a pet-sitting service is certainly a factor in income potential. A heavily populated urban area will naturally provide a greater number of customers than a rural setting. A part-time sitting service will not generate as much income as a full-time service. And a pet sitter working alone will not generate as much revenue as would a staff of busy pet sitters.

Another important ingredient in the income potential of a pet-sitting service is the personality of the owner. A business owner who does nothing but print up some business cards and sit by the phone will find herself only dreaming of income. A business owner who commits herself to the success of her business and then actively and aggressively pursues this commitment has a better chance of realizing a high income.

The chapters in this book on advertising and public relations will provide you with excellent ways to assertively and aggressively promote your pet-sitting business; however, it is up to you to follow through with the implementation.

I can give you some information that will help you to make your own income projections when assessing pet sitting as a career. A 2003 national survey of pet sitters indicates that the national average for a pet-sitting visit is approximately $15. Using this national average, you can determine the number of pet-sitting visits you anticipate making daily, weekly, monthly, and yearly. (If you plan to hire a staff of pet sitters, you'll need to project their visits as well.) Then, multiply this number by the average charge of $15 per visit to estimate your gross annual revenue. Of course, you'll need to estimate expenses that will be paid from your gross revenue to determine the income you will net, but this formula will give you a way of making income projections. After estimating how many daily visits are required for the yearly income you want to make, you'll need to set your marketing goals for how to achieve this level of business. In chapters 5 and 6 I will discuss several marketing and advertising techniques that will build your business (and revenues).

Although I can't tell you with any certainty what you, personally, can expect to earn through pet sitting, I can tell you that pet sitting has been profitable for me. My experience has shown that pet owners do not mind paying for peace of mind when they have to be away from home. I also can provide you with information and tools that will get you headed in the right direction for success!

WHAT YOU NEED TO START

Unlike many other business opportunities, pet sitting involves limited start-up costs. As of this edition of this book, I estimate that a professional pet-sitting service can be opened with a $3,000 to $5,000 investment, depending on the cost of living in your part of the country. (If you plan to pet sit on a small scale just for additional or secondary income, your start-up costs can be much less.)

Although you can spend a lot more, it really isn't necessary. After all, there is no costly inventory required, so your primary expenses will be for liability insurance, a dishonesty bond, office equipment, supplies, and professional services. And because pet sitting is an ideal home-based business, you can save money by not having to rent office space. (The details of how to open a pet-sitting service economically will be discussed in later chapters.)

Currently, pet sitting requires very little in the way of past experience or expertise. This may change in the near future though, because accreditation and certification programs are becoming available through national trade organizations. As the number of professional pet sitters increases, the additional education and training offered by such programs may become a distinguishing factor and a competitive edge among industry members.

As of this writing, these programs are strictly voluntary and there are no specific educational background requirements for pet sitters. However, any background in working with or caring for pets (even just for your own pets) will be a plus. In addition, any prior business courses or business experience are bound to be helpful.

I would say that the most important prerequisite of a pet sitter is that he or she needs to be a pet lover. Besides this, possessing good common sense, being responsible, reliable, honest, trustworthy, and having a sense of humor are the essential qualities needed for pet sitting.

Convinced that this business is for you? If so, the rest of this book is written to walk you through opening a professional and reputable pet-sitting service. I suggest you read it through for a general overview of what the profession entails. Then go back and concentrate on specific chapters as you proceed with your own pet-sitting business.

If you're already pet sitting professionally, there is much information in this book that may give you ideas on how to improve your existing business.

Chapter 2

Getting Started

Today's new entrepreneur has a wealth of information and resources available that will assist and explain how to start a small business. It's important to spend time seeking out these resources so that you can learn as much as possible before opening your pet-sitting service. I firmly believe that careful preliminary planning and research will contribute greatly to the success of your business venture. "Doing your homework" is what I call this imperative first step.

RESEARCH AND RESOURCES

Of course, reading this book is one of the wisest things you can do to understand the intricacies of a pet-sitting business. Unlike general business books, this one takes a hands-on approach specifically to running a pet-sitting service. I only wish my book had been available to me when I was thinking about and researching the field of pet sitting!

Nonetheless, you should check out other resources. Business books have become very popular—you'll find multitudes of them at your local bookstore and library, and on the Internet. These books and web sites will explain how to write a business plan (there is even a book, *The Pet Sitter's Business Plan*, that has a sample business plan for a pet-sitting business; see the appendix for ordering information), ways to raise business capital, and accounting practices for small businesses, among other things. Because of the wide availability of this sort of general information, I intentionally left out some of these subjects or skimmed over them in this book, but that does not mean these topics don't deserve your attention.

While visiting your local library or bookstore, spend some time perusing business magazines as well. There are many on the market today that contain informative articles on business start-ups, success stories, and important considerations for the small business owner. The trend toward self-employment in recent years has created an increase in publications for entrepreneurs, many of which provide useful information. Research should also include a search of your library's periodical files or web site archives for past articles on pet sitting (some of which are found in pet magazines), small businesses, and home-based ventures.

If you're thinking of operating your business from your home, first check with your city or county inspections department for ordinances and restrictions governing home businesses. You should also ascertain whether a home-occupation permit is required (usually there is a small charge for this permit). At the local level, you should research city or county ordinances that specifically apply to pets and animals. Are there leash laws or litter laws in effect? As a reputable pet sitter, you want to be aware of, and in compliance with, any such ordinances.

The Small Business Administration

The United States Small Business Administration (SBA) is a tremendous resource, and I strongly recommend that you contact your local SBA office for help researching or starting your business. Online you'll find their web site helpful, with easy-to-understand information. You'll be amazed at the wealth of information and assistance available from this government office. Your tax dollars help fund this organization, so why not take advantage of it? Write, call, or check their web site to get contact information of a field office in your area.

United States Small Business Administration
1111 Eighteenth Street, N.W., Sixth Floor
Washington, DC 20036
(202) 606-4000
www.sba.gov/

Through the SBA, you can receive training and guidance on everything from the basics of starting a small business and developing records and bookkeeping systems to locating sources of financing, finding customers, and determining a business site. The SBA also offers informative business development publications such as "Accounting Services for Small Service Firms," "Pricing Your Products and Services Profitably," "Planning and Goal Setting for Small Businesses," "Business Plan for Small Service Firms," and "Checklist for Going into Business." These are only a few of the many publications available; you should obtain and digest as much basic business knowledge as you can from these offerings. Some are available free of charge; there is a nominal charge for others. All are certainly of value to the budding entrepreneur.

You also can find excellent help from retired area executives who work through the SBA in a program called SCORE (Service Corps of Retired Executives). These retirees work as volunteers to help or mentor those who need assistance and counseling in the world of business. The SCORE program has been operating since 1965 and is an asset to any community because of the invaluable expertise it provides. The best part about it is that it's free! Check with your local SBA to determine if there is a SCORE group near you. A valuable service on the SBA web site is that you can submit business questions online for answers by SCORE volunteers.

Taxes

A resource that is a must for anyone thinking of starting a business is the Internal Revenue Service (IRS). Their web site, www.IRS.gov, is full of important information for business owners. If you don't have access to the Internet, call or visit your local IRS office to obtain publications that explain the types of business structures available (sole proprietor, partnership, corporation), the types of taxes that must be paid by businesses, what an Employer Identification Number (EIN) is, and how to apply for one. Accounting and bookkeeping systems are also discussed. This is mandatory reading for the new entrepreneur, so make sure checking with the IRS is on your to-do list.

> **Tip**
>
> Failure to withhold, collect, and pay required taxes can result in back tax assessments, along with interest and penalties. Become as knowledgeable as you can about these important aspects of running a business.

Your state tax department may have similar information available regarding state requirements for business owners. State taxes may include income, unemployment, and sales tax. Most states do not tax personal services, such as pet sitting, but this is not true in every state.

Another interesting web site is www.business.gov. You'll find frequently asked questions about small business matters that will help you wade through government rules and regulations you need to be concerned with, depending upon the type of business you'll be running (no employees, with employees, etc.).

Your Local Chamber of Commerce

Check to see if your chamber of commerce provides a Small Business Center or a volunteer program similar to SCORE. Also, request demographics of your local population, average income, and so on. Inquire about mentoring programs, business seminars, or workshops available to chamber of commerce members. Get the phone numbers for any local retail merchants' associations and your area's Better Business Bureau, then call them to learn about the information and services they provide.

Local Technical or Community Colleges

These often have a Small Business Center or Business Extension Department that offers business courses through their continuing education department. Classes or workshops can include everything from the basics of running a small business to the psychology behind consumer choices. Sometimes local experts, such as accountants or lawyers, are available as guest speakers and will answer questions from attendees.

I've taken advantage of several of these programs over the years. Some have been better than others, but all have been economical opportunities to learn. Plus, the classes were full of supportive entrepreneurial soul mates, some of whom became clients of my pet-sitting business after meeting me in class!

Other Pet Sitters

Now that our industry has been around a little while, some veteran pet sitters provide business consultation services (some consult for free, others charge a fee) for those thinking of getting into pet sitting. These pet sitters have a wealth of experience to share and care enough about their chosen career that they want newcomers to get started on the right foot. Contact information for pet sitters who offer consultation services is available from Pet Sitters International (see the appendix).

There are several groups of pet sitters who network locally. If any pet-sitting services exist in your community, call them to determine if they have networking meetings. Attending local meetings of pet sitters is an excellent way to learn about the business and to see if anyone local is interested in mentoring you. Pet Sitters International also maintains a listing of networking groups, so the organization may be able to tell you if a group currently meets in your area.

Trade Organizations

Last but certainly not least, trade organizations are a very valuable resource, and today it seems there is an organization for every profession under the sun! Of possible interest to small business owners are the National Association for the Self-Employed (NASE) and the National Federation of Independent Businesses (NFIB). Female entrepreneurs may find the National Foundation of Women Business Owners (NFWBO) to be a source of information. (Please see the appendix for contact information.)

Until I got into business for myself, I did not realize how helpful trade organizations are or how valuable they can be to an industry. Although there wasn't any such organization for pet sitters until I founded one in 1989, it (along with this book!) is something else that I wish had been available to me starting out. That's why I encourage new or wannabe pet sitters to immediately contact Pet Sitters International, an educational organization for professional pet sitters.

PET SITTERS INTERNATIONAL

What does a trade organization do that makes it so valuable to industry members? Much more than the public probably realizes. I was somewhat ignorant myself until, as a business owner, I became aware of needs in this industry that weren't being met. So, assuming that you are not aware of the importance of an industry association, I'd like to spend a little time enlightening you about the benefits and services available to pet-sitting industry members through Pet Sitters International (PSI).

First, understand that there is clout (power and influence) in numbers. Having an industry organization in place that comprises many industry members is impressive, not only because it lends credibility to a profession, but also because numbers get people's attention. Having a trade organization has helped us educate the pet-owning consumers we want as clients and make them understand about the wide availability of our services in the United States and Canada.

It has also helped us get the recognition we deserve from related businesses and industries. For example, we now have a tailor-made business liability insurance policy available to our members. Today's pet sitter doesn't have to put up with the frustration many of us endured while trying to find this important coverage for our businesses. The best part is that the insurance is offered to us at affordable group rates—because through our organization, we are a professional group!

Another stride we have made as an organized group involves the Yellow Pages of many phone directories. Years ago, there were so few of us and the industry was so new that most Yellow Page companies made us list our businesses under the heading "Kennels." Although this was not all bad, it still did not give us the professional distinction we were working so hard to establish. (Our educational efforts were telling pet owners to try a pet sitter, yet, when they consulted the Yellow Pages for such a service, we weren't listed where people would think to look!) So a major letter-writing campaign was conducted to Yellow Pages publishers, which resulted in new Yellow Pages headings for many of our members.

These examples might not seem like much, but they have been great accomplishments for our new industry—important steps that have helped us to evolve into the professional, credible, and viable industry that pet sitting is today. Such accomplishments translate into time- and money-saving victories for today's new pet sitter.

Support is another benefit that comes from a trade organization. Member services include client referrals, quality standards, and news releases pertaining to industry trends and developments. In assessing the value of organizations such as PSI, one has to look at the big picture: Each time PSI participates in a radio, TV, newspaper, or magazine interview, it provides publicity for the profession, which enhances opportunities for all pet sitters. Each time we're able to negotiate a special rate for our members, it shows that our industry's business is recognized and coveted for its purchasing power. Equally as important, members can run their businesses more confidently knowing that PSI is there for them and is working to help make their pet-sitting business a success.

Education is a very valuable benefit as well. From PSI, pet sitters receive an enormous amount of information that deals specifically with professional pet sitting. Through a bimonthly magazine, *The World of Professional Pet Sitting*, an annual convention, and a forum on the web site, members have several venues within which to share experiences, tips, and concerns. The camaraderie and networking that takes place among members is, itself, often worth the price of membership.

The pet-sitting industry has come a long way since 1994, when Pet Sitters International was founded to support, promote, and recognize excellence in pet sitting. Through PSI, the industry now recognizes its best in an annual Pet Sitter of the Year award and celebrates the profession during Professional Pet Sitters Week (the first full week of March each year). PSI also holds an internationally known annual event, Take Your Dog to Work Day, which celebrates the great companions dogs are and encourages their adoption.

Today's pet sitters are very fortunate to have PSI, as well as many other resources, available to them. Use all you can to operate your pet-sitting service efficiently, effectively, and successfully.

A MARKET SURVEY

While doing your preliminary business research, you're bound to see this step mentioned in other general business books. It's a sound business step and is worth emphasizing here. To some extent, the need for personalized, at-home pet care exists in all communities; by conducting a marketing survey, you can ascertain what interest there is in your local area. There are many ways to conduct such a survey. A good way to begin is to check the local Yellow Pages under "Kennels," "Pet Sitters," "Sitting Services," or "Dog/Cat Exercising" to determine if any other pet-sitting services already operate in your city or county. If not, you can be fairly confident there is a need for this type of business.

You can better determine the level of interest or need by calling local veterinarians, groomers, and pet supply store owners. Tell them about your plans, see if they know of anyone else offering such a service (some pet sitters don't advertise), and ask if they think this type of pet care would be well received by their clients (also ask how many clients they have!). While you have their attention, ask if they would support your efforts by telling pet owners about your services once you're up and running. Offer a reciprocal referral arrangement with them.

If there is another pet sitter offering their services, call and ask to speak with the person. *Be honest* and explain you're considering entering the field. The pet sitter may provide valuable insight as to how busy their service is, whether they must turn down business, and the areas in which they work. Ask if the pet sitter might help you get started for a consultation fee. Remember, time and expertise are valuable commodities. A personal consultation with an experienced pet sitter may be worth its weight in gold.

Please do yourself and the industry a favor when calling other pet sitters by being honest. Many people today have caller ID, which tells them from what number a call is coming. I've heard from several pet sitters who were incensed that competitors posing as clients had called to ask questions about how their services are run. Often a seasoned pet sitter can tell just by the nature of the questions who is on the other end of the line. Old-fashioned honesty and trustworthiness are crucial in the pet-sitting business, so it's far better to start out right and earn the respect of your colleagues by stating who you are and the purpose of your call. The worst thing that can happen is that the pet sitter will hang up on you, but the start of good rapport and a cooperative relationship could be the outcome.

Returning to your market survey, you'll next want to approach pet owners and get their reaction to your proposed business. Find out how often they travel and what they currently do with their pets when they must leave home. Try to determine if they would be receptive to your service. Ask how much they'd be willing to pay for in-home care and what they'd expect from such a service.

Tip

Cooperative working relationships among local pet sitters have become very typical. This is because we've seen a trend in the industry of one- to two-person pet-sitting services (husband and wife teams, friends, sisters, and so on). Although these businesses could grow and expand, they are intentionally choosing to remain small to keep a more personal slant to the business and to avoid the headaches that can sometimes be associated with managing personnel. But since every pet sitter needs time off and an emergency backup, pet sitters are finding it beneficial to maintain good working relationships so they can fill in for one another during times of illness, emergency, or vacation. This is where local networking really pays off, because it enables you to get to know other pet sitters and feel comfortable about those to whom you refer or share clients.

Pet sitters may also realize advantages in working together at the local level by advertising cooperatively, holding fund-raisers for community animal organizations, or simply meeting for lunch occasionally. After all, no one understands this unique business like another pet sitter.

You can conduct this portion of your survey by cold-calling people from the telephone book and asking if they own a pet. You could obtain permission from a shopping center to approach a random group of shoppers with your questions. A better way, though, is to acquire a list of clients (including addresses and telephone numbers) from a veterinarian or groomer or even from tax or license listings of dog or cat owners. Another option is to see if your local grocery store sells client information. Now that most grocers are using "reward card" programs, they have information on file about customers' buying habits. See if you can purchase contact information on clients who buy pet food, kitty litter, and the like. Because these people already own pets, it is a far more efficient way to conduct your research.

One pet sitter I know purchased a mailing list from a pet magazine of subscribers in her city. She then sent out an initial customer query form to these prospective customers, informing them of her new business venture and inquiring about their interest in using her services. She included a preprinted, stamped postcard that enabled them to quickly answer her questions and register their pet(s) with her company for future sittings. Not only did she receive lots of encouraging comments, but she got several definite customers before she even opened for business.

While doing your market research, don't forget to canvass your friends as well. You can usually count on friends to be honest because they want you to be happy and successful. They'll tell you if they think your idea is a good one, if the concept will go over in your area, and if they think you're cut out for this type of work. Invite their opinions and then listen objectively.

Offer your pet-sitting services free of charge to a few pet-owning friends. Let them see firsthand the quality of services you plan to provide and then give them the chance to critique you. These trial runs will be a wise investment of your time, plus you'll have some references to use when the general public starts calling.

Once you've conducted your market survey, analyzed the results, done some gratis pet sitting, and received honest feedback from friends or family members, you can more knowledgeably and confidently determine if a pet-sitting business is needed in your community—and if it's the right business for you.

Take good notes on the information and the statistics you gather during this survey. They may be useful in writing a business plan—especially if you'll be borrowing any operating capital to get your business started.

NAMING YOUR BUSINESS

Selecting a name for your pet-sitting service is an important first step. Put your thinking cap on—this task is not as easy as you might imagine. Keep in mind that the name of your business creates a crucial first impression. Make sure the name you choose conveys a positive image with which you'll be proud to be associated.

Selecting a name has become a more difficult task in recent years. When I opened my pet-sitting service in 1983, there were so few services in operation that I had a wide choice of cute, catchy names available to me. Today, with the increasing number of new pet-sitting businesses, some names are trademarked and are therefore totally off-limits. That's why it's a good idea to come up with several names for your business. If your first choice is not available, you'll be ready with other options.

Once you've narrowed down your name selections to two or three favorites, you'll need to check with your local Register of Deeds to see if your first choice is in use by another business in your community. If the name is locally available to you, your next inquiry should be to the Secretary of State's office to determine if anyone in your state has registered a business under your preferred name. If not, you'll probably have free and clear right to do business under that name in your state.

At this point, the only hitch with being able to use the name is if it has already been trademarked with the United States Patent and Trademark Office (PTO) in Washington, D.C. You can determine if there's a federal trademark on the name by visiting the U.S. Patent and Trademark Office's web site (www.uspto.gov) and checking registrations, or by hiring a patent and trademark attorney to do this verification for you.

Although hiring an attorney to make sure you have the right to use a business name can involve some expense, this can be a wise initial investment. I know of one pet sitter in Florida who had been doing business under a certain name for more than a year. She had established an excellent reputation and developed a devoted clientele. Out of the blue one day, a letter arrived from an attorney in the Midwest informing her to cease and desist use of her business's name immediately because it was federally trademarked by his client. To make a long story short, the Florida pet sitter had to hire an attorney to look into the matter, only to find that indeed, she did not have the right to do business under her current name. Her innocent mistake ended up being a very costly one. It was expensive to change all of her forms, stationery, and business literature. Having to notify her clients of a new name was awkward as well. She told me it would have been much cheaper to go through all the proper name-checking channels at the outset—not to mention the headaches she would have been spared.

Once you've decided on a name and made sure it is available, consider how you can best protect the name for your business. Discuss how to do this with an attorney, because it's a very serious subject. With the anticipated continued growth of the pet-sitting industry, you don't want any surprises in your mailbox in the years to come. And you'll want the legal backing to be able to protect your good name and reputation if another pet sitter tries to infringe upon it.

One way to begin protecting your business name is to go to your local Register of Deeds office and register the name as a business in your community. There will be a nominal charge for the registration.

YOUR BUSINESS LOGO

Many business owners like to develop an identifiable signature or trademark for their company. A logo can be simply a set of letters, or it can include graphics. Think of the McDonald's golden arches, the distinctive Coca-Cola script, or the red bull's-eye for Target stores. These are all logos.

If you want to establish a logo for your pet-sitting service, consider doing so at the outset. There are two reasons for developing your logo early. First, if you plan to federally trademark your name, it may be wise to trademark the logo along with it. Second, it's cost-effective to have the logo printed on your company materials from the start, rather than adding it later.

If you're creative and skilled in using a computer, you can design your own logo using one of the many software programs that offer clip art (art that is copyright free). Consider hiring a graphic artist or aspiring art student in your area to develop a logo for your business. Use the logo on all of your company literature and advertising to create a distinctive professional image for your business.

> ### *Tip*
>
> Please be aware of copyright and trademark laws when designing a logo. In other words, don't think you can use the McDonald's golden arches for your company's logo, nor can you copy something from a book, magazine, or web site just because you like it.

BUSINESS LICENSE

Your next step will be to check with your city and county offices to determine if a license to do business is required. Most communities issue these licenses for a small fee and a little paperwork; some require that the license be visibly displayed in your place of business. Remember that if you'll be operating a home-based pet-sitting service, you may need a home occupation permit before a city/county business license will be issued to you.

As an upstanding citizen running a legitimate business, you'll need to obtain the proper business license(s) for your pet-sitting service. If you're unsure where to find out what is necessary in the way of licenses, check your local telephone directory under "Government" or "City/County" headings for the appropriate offices.

Please understand that a city/county business license is simply a tax-generating permit authorizing you to do business in your area. It in no way indicates your knowledge or abilities as a professional pet sitter. However, through the years there has been a trend by some pet sitters to list this business license as a credential on their business cards and company literature. This has become a pet peeve of mine—I think it is misleading to the public. Usually when we see the term "licensed," we think of a state exam or course of study being required in order to obtain the license. Because, as of this writing, there is no regulatory licensing required of professional pet sitters, using the term is misleading.

There is now a voluntary accreditation program available to pet sitters through PSI that does involve a self-paced home study program with a proctored test that must be passed for certification. This is a much more meaningful business credential with which to honestly impress the general public.

YOUR OFFICE LOCATION

You will need to determine the location for your pet-sitting service. The service, especially in the beginning, can easily be run from your home (if, as discussed earlier, home-based businesses are permitted in your area). A spare bedroom, a section of the basement, or even a walk-in closet may be adequate. You only need a small space to set up your operation. In the past, there have been tax advantages to operating a business from home. Because tax laws change frequently, get advice from a tax professional concerning the advantages of operating a business from your home.

If the idea of basing your business in your home appeals to you, give careful thought to whether you can work well at home. Can you discipline yourself to work, or will there be too many distractions and temptations to keep you from giving your business the time and effort required? Also, a large part of a pet-sitting service is conducted over the telephone, and calls can come at all hours. To keep work from disrupting your home life, you will have to be able to separate these two areas and think of the office as a workplace with its own hours.

Will you be running your pet-sitting service alone, or will you have a partner who will share the workload? If you have a partner, this may be a factor in determining where your office is located. A partner or office assistant may not feel comfortable or be able to work efficiently from your home. Will other pet-sitting staff members be traipsing in and out of your home? This could be bothersome to other family members and could result in complaints from neighbors

---

Tip

Running a business from home and not treating it as a business from the start has quickly led to burnout for more than one pet sitter. It's very important to set policies and operating procedures—such as the hours when you'll answer your business phone and return calls—and then stick to them as you would for a job based outside of your home. The convenience of working from home can be lost if you feel like you never get to leave the business. Be aware of this pitfall and implement measures to ensure you control your business, as opposed to it controlling you!

---

as well. Do you have small children who may decide to throw a tantrum while you're trying to sell your services? Give careful thought to your office location at the outset. Be sure of your location before having your business address and phone number printed on any material; making changes on printed literature can be expensive.

If you can work out the details and base your business in your home, it can be convenient and usually much cheaper. In fact, the establishment of home-based businesses of all types is a fast-growing phenomenon as more and more people discover the advantages of working at home. According to IDC, a top national research firm, as of 2002 there were more than 20 million home-based businesses in the United States.

If you prefer to locate your business outside your home, remember that you do not need the plushest surroundings for office space. All you need at the beginning is an area large enough to accommodate a desk (or card table) for your phone and computer, and a bookcase or shelf (or another card table) for your supplies, files, and resource materials. It is rare for a customer to visit your office, so appearances are not critical. Look for the most reasonable rent in a convenient and safe area of town where you'll look forward to working. A final word of advice: Remember that rents and lease terms are not carved in stone. Don't be afraid to negotiate—you might find that a landlord is willing to be flexible to secure a good tenant.

BASIC OFFICE SUPPLIES AND FURNISHINGS

You'll need a few basic furnishings and supplies for your business office before officially opening your pet-sitting service. Try to keep your office needs to a minimum to reduce your overhead costs. You can pass on these savings to your customers in lower pet-sitting rates. (Lower rates may result in a higher volume of customers, which will contribute to the success of your business.) Recommended office basics include:

- Table or desk

- Chair(s)

- Bookcase (shelf or space for supplies)

- Telephone (see the "Business Telephone" section in this chapter)

- Telephone answering machine or answering service

- City map (one for the office and one for your car—a city map is helpful for determining service routes, as well as for getting you to your clients' homes)

- Calculator (a basic model that adds, subtracts, multiplies, and divides should suffice—one with paper tape comes in handy when adding deposits)

- Name and address rubber stamp (handy for endorsing checks and pre-addressing envelopes for customers to use when paying—don't forget the necessary ink pad)

- Typewriter, word processor, or computer

- Filing cabinet (a must for storing paperwork such as service contracts, forms, and advertising that is associated with your business; if you'll be storing client house keys or confidential information such as alarm codes, get one with a lock)

- Schedule book and calendar or Palm Pilot (a way to keep up with customer appointments, sitting assignments, and the rest of life is absolutely necessary! Write everything down, or you'll find yourself needing to pick up two sets of house keys at the same time on opposite ends of town . . . which is very hard to do.)

Tip

A typewriter or computer is nice but is not absolutely necessary. If you don't have access to one, or don't type, you can hire a typist (look in the classified ads of your newspaper or in the Yellow Pages). You can also have any necessary forms typeset at a printing company or buy them from a pet-sitting supply company.

● Reference books and educational videos on various pets and their care (some of these may be available from your local library or similar information may be found on web sites. Familiarize yourself with different types of animals and various breeds. When a customer calls and asks what you charge for caring for a Maltese, you'll know it's a dog and not a falcon!)

● First-aid supplies for humans (bandages for paper cuts!) and pet emergencies

You will need the following paper supplies:

● Index cards and storage box

● Stationery (professionally printed with your business name, address, phone number, and any logo or slogan you want to associate with your business)

● Envelopes matching your stationery (you may want to pick a color scheme and use it everywhere your name is seen; the repetition will help make your business recognizable to your public)

● Plain envelopes (white business envelopes you can address with your rubber stamp to leave for your customers to remit payment)

● Plain paper (to put into your computer's printer)

● Business cards (get these professionally printed because you will use them a lot to advertise your business; they are relatively inexpensive and you want them to look nice and to convey a good first impression to potential clients)

● A flyer or brochure that gives basic information about what your service provides (this is a valuable advertising tool you'll use often, and is discussed in more detail in chapter 5)

● Notepads (plain or matching your other stationery; you will use these primarily for leaving your clients notes and, of course, for phone messages)

● Accounting ledger (this is a columnar book that your accountant will most likely supply and explain to you, unless you are using a computer software program for your bookkeeping)

● Five-column accounting pad (this ledger is available in most office supply stores. The sheets contain lined pages you can use to chart sitter schedules. You can also find scheduling functions in some pet-sitting software programs.)

● Business forms (you will need at least a carefully thought out service contract for your business, and other forms will be helpful as well; these are discussed further in chapter 8)

Other standard office supplies you'll need include:

- Pens and pencils

- Scissors

- Ruler

- Tape

- Postage stamps

- Labels for folders and house keys

- Paper clips

- Stapler

- File folders

- Staple remover

- Hanging file folders

- Correction fluid (handy for changing information on service contracts)

Your office supplies need not be brand new. If you have an extra pair of scissors around the house, loan them to your business. For anything you purchase for your business, make sure you keep the receipt. Any legitimate office and business expenses will need to be accounted for at tax time.

Keep your business supplies as pet-related as possible. Your logo, stationery, and business cards, for example, can easily be designed to reflect the nature of your business. Try to order checks that have pets or wildlife pictured on them. Also, purchase stamps that feature pets or wildlife. I used such checks and stamps for years and found that people really did notice the coordinated details of my business. Just be sure not to sacrifice professionalism for what I call "cutesiness."

Although your clients will furnish most of the things you'll need to properly care for their pet(s), there are some recommended supplies that will be helpful in the course of actually pet sitting. These are detailed in chapter 4, in the "Sitter Orientation" and "Survival Items" sections.

BUSINESS TELEPHONE

Some pet sitters operating from home have made the mistake of using their personal telephone number as their business line. This is not a good idea, for several reasons:

• Your telephone company will not appreciate your disregard for any policy they may have regarding business lines. There could even be a tariff violation or penalty if it learns of your home-based business.

• Although a business line does normally cost more than a residential line, you also usually get a free Yellow Pages listing for your business. This exposure can really help increase the calls you'll receive for service. After all, if you've named your business "XYZ Pet Sitters" but your phone number is only listed under your name, Mary Doe, how is the public going to find you? Your credibility as a reputable business could be damaged by a potential client's inability to find your number in the phone book or through directory information.

• As your business grows, your phone will be ringing more and more. Calls will come in at all hours. Because you'll have no way of knowing whether the call is personal or business, you'll find yourself answering the phone and possibly beginning to feel that you have no privacy. Prevent this problem by ordering a legitimate business line from the start. That way, you can distinguish callers and answer your business line only during your regularly scheduled office hours.

• Your business phone bill will be an expense of doing business and, as such, can be claimed on your income tax return. By having a separate bill for your business line, your record and receipt keeping will also be a much easier task.

You may be wondering if you'll need either a telephone answering machine/voice mail system or a personal answering service for your business. Yes! You will need one of these methods for taking messages. The merits of each are discussed further in the next chapter.

> ### *Tip*
>
> Many customers will want to memorize your business phone number. Get a number that you plan to keep for years and one that's easy to remember as well. Have the entire phone number or the last four digits spell out PETS or DOGS or CATS or LOVE—something identifiable with your service!

STRUCTURING YOUR BUSINESS

Another important consideration in starting your pet-sitting service is how to legally structure your business. The choices available include sole proprietorship, general partnership or limited partnership, corporation (C corporation and S corporation), and limited liability company (LLC). Tax consequences and liabilities vary with each of these legal structures. Seek advice from professionals (attorney, accountant, tax consultant) before deciding which structure is the best for you and your business.

It is entirely possible to determine your business's legal structure and incorporate your business (if that is your choice) by yourself, just as you can do the research and leg work to register your business's name and obtain business licenses. This way you save attorney fees and lower your start-up costs. However, I strongly recommend that you at least consult with an attorney regarding these business matters and decisions. Usually the charge is small for such a consultation, and the discussion will help you make informed decisions about your business. A reliable attorney or accountant can be important in your business's well-being. You are wise to cultivate good relationships with both at the very outset of your new venture. In other words, let key people do what they do best to help you do your best.

FINDING AN ACCOUNTANT

Here again, unless you're an experienced bookkeeper, it is advisable to find an accountant to assist you with the necessary record keeping for your pet-sitting service. Look for one who specializes in accounting for small businesses.

An accountant will help you set up your books, do your payroll, and apply for any necessary identification numbers. An accountant can also save you some running around by supplying the forms you'll need, such as state and federal payroll tax forms. Although accounting procedures may at first seem overwhelming to a new business owner, a good accountant will soon have you trained and knowledgeable about the financial side of your business.

Shop around when searching for an accountant. Ask other small business owners for recommendations and then interview a few accountants before making a decision. Accounting fees and expertise vary, so don't be shy about asking for fee information, credentials, and references from candidates.

Make sure the individual is someone you feel you can trust and with whom you can get along. If you find yourself unhappy with an accountant, remember that you are not locked into their services and you can take your business elsewhere.

SELECTING A BANK

A business checking account is necessary for your pet-sitting service. Here again, it pays to shop around before making a decision. Different banks offer various features and hours of operation. You should take into account the convenience of the bank's location. Once your pet-sitting services become popular, you'll have little time to waste when making bank deposits. Some banks advertise specifically to attract small business owners. Find out what, if any, services they provide that may directly benefit you.

Explore the possibility of obtaining a credit card exclusively for your business's use. In today's business world, a credit card can come in handy when making large purchases for your business, traveling to workshops and conventions, or simply entertaining clients or staff members. Also, by paying your account on time, the credit card helps you establish a credit history for your business.

Will the bank extend you a line of credit or overdraft protection? This can be important to sustain you during any lull in business or to help you invest in your business with things such as advertising campaigns or computer equipment.

Also find out whether the bank will issue a merchant card to you. This enables you to accept Visa and MasterCard from clients as payment for services. Although in the past most pet sitters have only accepted cash or personal checks, there is an increasing trend in the industry, especially among larger pet-sitting companies, to accept charge cards for payment. There are advantages and disadvantages to accepting plastic, so obtain details from your banker so you can carefully consider this option for your business.

Allot the proper amount of time to explore banking services for your business, even down to the details of what type of checks and deposit slips are available. (Many pet sitters like to order animal- or pet-theme checks to use in their business.) It's important to spend this time during your planning stages, because after your business is up and running your time truly does become more limited.

INSURANCE

It is smart and advisable to obtain liability insurance to cover you and any other pet sitters working in your business. Actually, I strongly encourage you not to go into business without this coverage, and after you read "Don't Do This!" in chapter 7, I think you'll agree. Hopefully, you'll never need to use this insurance, but having the coverage will give you and your customers peace of mind. A very important consideration is that it is often a selling point to interested but hesitant customers.

After the first edition of this book came out, many people contacted me to say that they had a difficult time finding commercial liability insurance for their pet-sitting businesses. I could empathize with them because I, too, had a difficult time obtaining such insurance when I first opened my service. The reason it was difficult to find coverage is that pet sitting was a relatively new profession with unique insurance needs. A pet-sitting business is unlike a kennel operation that insures its premises for accidents and damages. Instead, a pet sitter needs protection that insures the premises of each client where he or she is conducting business. Our need is similar to that of a janitorial or cleaning service that visits various locations to perform its duties. However, our liability coverage also needs to extend to the animals entrusted to our care.

Even today, some insurance companies may still say they have never heard of the pet-sitting industry and, therefore, won't have a policy already available to meet your specific needs. Although this doesn't mean an insurance policy cannot be created that is tailored to your business, you need to be prepared to explain the nature of the pet-sitting business and ask if a policy can be designed specifically for you. If you have an insurance agent with whom you've done business in the past, contact them first for help in this area. If they've written automobile or homeowner's insurance for you, they know a little about you. To keep your business, they may be more willing to seek out the proper coverage that meets the needs of your pet-sitting business.

Be sure any policy you consider provides "care, custody, and control" coverage. Most business liability policies exclude this type of coverage, but it is exactly what pet sitters need.

Still, it's going to be hard to beat the Pet Sitters Liability Protection Policy that was written for pet sitters and is offered, at group rates, through PSI. I strongly advise pet sitters to take advantage of this plan. The plan has now been available to PSI members for more than ten years and the insurer has a great service record and knowledge of our industry's needs. It saves you time in locating good coverage and it saves you money by being a group plan.

Car Insurance

Another insurance concern you should look into is your automobile coverage. Because you'll most likely be doing a lot more driving as a professional pet sitter, find out if your car insurance is adequate. Many pet sitters purchase an insurance rider that provides additional coverage in case they get into an accident while pet sitting. This type of coverage is triggered only if the pet sitter's personal automobile insurance coverage is not adequate for damages incurred. This coverage can be very important if you will have a staff of pet sitters working for your company. Find out if your company's rider will extend to their vehicles, just in case. We do live in a lawsuit-mad society!

Worker's Compensation

If you'll be hiring employees to help you with pet-sitting visits, you'll also need to investigate Worker's Compensation insurance in your state. Most states require some form of this insurance, and your personal insurance agent or state Department of Labor can tell you what applies to your business. This type of insurance covers the employees of a business if they are injured while working.

Life and Disability Insurance

As your business grows, you should review your life insurance coverage. Make sure it would be sufficient to keep your business going in the event of your death and that it would cover any debts owed by your business for which your estate

---

Tip

States classify workers by assigning a code to them, which is then used to assign Worker's Compensation rates to various occupations. The 2005 edition of the *National Council of Compensation Insurance Scopes Manual* established a near-universal class code. Pet sitters now all fall under the code 0917 Domestic Contractor. Rates will vary depending on the state, but code is applicable in all states except Arizona, California, Indiana, and Michigan. These four states have a state-specific code. Some insurance agents who are not using an *NCCI Scopes Manual* may try to classify a pet sitting business differently, but according to the agency that issues the Pet Sitters Liability Policy through Pet Sitters International, 0917 is the correct class for our industry.

may be accountable. Life insurance may not have been important to you before, but it is something you should consider as a business owner.

Disability insurance is another product you should give thought to. What happens when you're self-employed as a pet sitter and something occurs that makes you unable to work for several weeks or months?

Sometimes people going into business for themselves scrimp on this type of protection to save money when they're first starting out. The need for pursuing this coverage early on was brought out by my friend Kerri, who had spent several years building a terrific business. Around the start of her fourth year, she was diagnosed with multiple sclerosis. Her ensuing battle with this debilitating disease has forced her to drastically scale back her pet sitting and has sidelined her for several periods of unemployment. And of course, now that she has been diagnosed with this disease, she does not qualify for disability insurance. Not wanting others to find themselves unable to work and with no means of income, she always asks me to tell pet sitters about the importance of disability insurance. Many companies offer short-term and long-term disability plans. Do as Kerri advises and spend some time exploring these programs while you're in the process of getting started.

> ### Tip
>
> While researching your insurance needs, do some cost comparisons—coverage and rates can vary among insurance companies. Besides, each phone call you make will help educate more insurance agents about our growing industry. And who knows? The agent may be a local pet owner who would be interested in using your service!

DISHONESTY BOND

Many people are familiar with the term "bonded," but few understand what it really means. Because it is just as important to the professional pet sitter as having good liability insurance, I want to take a few minutes to discuss bonding.

Simply defined, a bond is a form of insurance that protects the business owner (and, in pet sitting, the customer) in the event of theft. However, unlike insurance, if a bond company makes payment, it usually expects restitution of the amount paid either from the business owner or the convicted party. From whom the restitution is expected is very important to you, as a business owner, in purchasing a bond. If you plan to hire staff pet sitters in your business, you'll sleep much better knowing that if one of your pet sitters is convicted of theft, your bond will reimburse your client (up to the amount payable by your bond). Your bonding company will then go after the convicted pet sitter to recoup the money it paid for the theft. Make sure this is the type of bond you purchase— you don't want the company to expect *you* to reimburse it for a loss due to someone else's actions.

This type of bond, recommended for pet sitters, is currently available from a respected surety company that works with members of PSI. This company has also provided a rider to PSI members who operate their business as sole proprietors. Although many bonding companies will not extend a bond to the owner of a business, this particular one has made an exception because so many pet-sitting firms are owner-operated.

How much of a bond should you consider purchasing for your pet-sitting business? This is a personal business decision. If you'll be working alone and doing all the pet-sitting visits yourself, you may want to purchase only a small bond in the amount of $5,000 or $10,000. (This assumes you know that you are honest and trustworthy, so you're only purchasing a minimum bond as a good faith effort for your business and as a selling point to clients.) If you plan to use a staff of pet sitters or if you pet sit in very affluent areas, a higher bond might be advisable.

A concern of new pet sitters that I often hear is, "What's to stop someone from setting me up and accusing me of stealing from their home just to collect some money?" This is a legitimate concern and one that worried me, too, at the outset. What you need to understand, though, is that it's not so easy to do. For a dishonesty bond to pay out, a person has to be tried and convicted of the crime—it takes more than just an accusation. Falsely accusing someone is not a pleasant, fast, or easy way to make some money.

> ### Tip
>
> As a business owner who is responsible for the pet sitters you send into customers' homes, you'll be wise to do thorough background checks to make sure the people you hire are honest, reliable, and trustworthy. Checking references is discussed in more detail in chapter 4.

Still, as the owner of a service business that visits strangers' homes, you'll be smart to go this extra step and take out a dishonesty bond. The cost is nominal when you consider the peace of mind it provides for you and your customers. And, being bonded and insured speaks well for the professionalism and integrity of your business and for our industry as a whole.

Chapter 3

Office Procedures

When I started my pet-sitting business in 1983, it was literally on a shoestring budget, with files kept in a shoebox and a card table for a desk. Computers at that time were enormous mainframes that required an entire room at large companies. When I decided to implement a newsletter for my pet sitters and later on one for my clients, these were pecked out on my trusty Smith-Corona typewriter that had served me well in college. Any graphics they contained were cut and pasted by hand.

It wasn't until the later years of running my pet-sitting business that personal computers began hitting the marketplace. Even then, though, there weren't any specialized software programs for pet-sitting businesses. It was a matter of taking general accounting programs and trying to adapt them to the needs of pet sitter schedules, client invoices, reservation information, and so on.

USING A COMPUTER

What a difference the personal computer and the Internet have made to the pet-sitting industry! The Internet alone has made it much easier to research various species and breeds that pet sitters are asked to care for, to communicate with clients and other pet sitters by e-mail, and to advertise services on business web sites.

At Pet Sitters International, one of the most popular benefits of membership is the Locator feature available on the PSI web site. This is where pet owners looking for a pet sitter can type in their home zip code and receive a list of PSI members who serve that area. Thousands of pet owners visit the PSI

Locator every month. Seven years ago, this valuable Locator didn't exist. Now, thanks to the numerous advances in technology, it's the way many pet owners find their pet sitter.

Do You Really Need One?

Before we discuss computers any further, just in case there are some of you reading this book who like me, are computer illiterate, I want to put your minds at ease by telling you that you don't have to use a computer to be a successful pet sitter. Especially if you plan to keep your business small and, say, pet sit for a few handfuls of pet owners in your neighborhood, subdivision, or retirement community, the index card system I first used (which I will describe later in this chapter) will work fine for you. Don't be put off doing something you think you'd really enjoy (pet sitting) because you think it has to involve something you have no interest in (computers).

But if you are even a little bit computer savvy and/or if you want to operate your pet-sitting business on a larger scale, then using a computer can have many advantages.

When they work, they're great! And today, with several software programs written specifically for the professional pet-sitting business, the administrative and accounting functions are easier than ever. Some software programs give your clients the option to check and update their scheduled visits and to pay by a secure server. Some programs enable your pet sitters to log on and check their personal schedule at any time, which can eliminate miscommunication and potential missed visits.

Having your records computerized enables you to monitor accounts receivable, reference a client's history in seconds, and track your referrals by pet type, zip code, or advertising method. You can store many types of letters in the computer, and then customize them in just a minute. You'll also be able to broadcast or communicate with your clients or pet sitters via "e-blasts" (mass e-mails) and even administer pre-screening tests to job applicants (see chapter 4).

There's no doubt about it, using a computer can help you to run your business more easily and efficiently. For a listing of pet-sitting software developers, please search the Internet for "pet sitting software programs" or contact Pet Sitters International.

Do You Need a Web Site?

While it once seemed questionable to me that a service as personal as pet sitting could sell itself over the Internet, now, due to the hectic schedules of pet owners and pet sitters, web sales have become a common way of doing business.

The typical pet-sitting client chooses our method of pet care not only for the personalization involved, but also for the convenience. Life today is just plain busy, so the opportunity to research pet-sitting services on the Internet, at one's leisure, can result in more serious inquiries for pet-sitting businesses that have web sites.

Similarly, today's pet sitters are out and about making pet-sitting visits and are not always accessible by phone. Having a web site as a first line of introduction and information can cut down time spent on return calls by answering many basic questions. While a display ad in the phone book's Yellow Pages can create awareness of your business, it usually costs more in the long run for less space to generate your message than does a web site.

Several pet sitters who are not at all computer savvy have told me (and proudly!) that they were able to set up their own web site by using templates available from hosting companies or by purchasing point-and-click software programs for building web pages.

Using a professional web site developer is also an option. They can usually offer more sophisticated design techniques with moving images and flash animation. Professional web site developers can be found in your phone book Yellow Pages, but also consider contacting community colleges or high schools in your area that offer computer classes. Computers are second nature to kids today, so you may find a student who will design a site for you for a nominal charge, or even for free, just because they love computers. A web site at reasonable design and hosting fees is also a membership benefit offered by Pet Sitters International. So when you're comparing your possibilities, be sure to look into it as well. For tips on what to include on your web site, see chapter 5.

Be aware that to have your own web site you will need to purchase a web domain name, such as www.MarysPetSitters.com, or www.wesitpets.net, or whatever else you can think of that hasn't already been taken by someone else. The going rate for a domain name as of this writing is $35 annually, and usually you must purchase the name for two years. Don't forget that the purchase of your domain name doesn't guarantee you the name forever! Be aware of your renewal date and try to renew rights to the domain name before they expire.

Who will host your site (where your web site is stored or placed for viewing on the web) is another decision you'll have to make, and this is an area where you'll want to do some research. Find out where the host company's computers are stored and what their track record is for their computers being "down" (which means your web site is unavailable for viewing!). What is their customer service and troubleshooting like? Ask for references of other businesses they work with.

It's generally believed to be better to go with a company whose sole job it is to host web sites. Most hosting companies are now charging $10 month and

---

Tip

Having the right to use a web site domain name is entirely separate from owning a business name through federal or state trademark law. Just because a web site domain registry gives you clearance to use www.WeSitPets.com doesn't mean that another business may not have the name We Sit Pets federally trademarked for their existing business. The two registrations are independent of each other.

My advice is to make sure your business's name is not used or owned by anyone in pet sitting before adopting it for your business. Since most of the time a business wants its web domain name to match or closely resemble its business name, check the availability as a domain name. Once your attorney has given you the green flag to proceed in both cases with the name, then go to the expense of registering the name and printing it on business materials.

---

there are many companies to choose from. If you use a professional web site designer, they can often recommend some to you, or if you go with the service offered by Pet Sitters International, the hosting is included in the program.

Pet Sitters International E-Age Survey

Because more than 90 percent of PSI members have e-mail addresses, the organization conducted an informal survey in 2004 to see how the electronic age was affecting member businesses. The survey results included (more survey results are shown in the box on page 49):

- 78 percent of pet sitters have a web site advertising their business; on average, 36 percent of their business comes from these web sites.

- 64 percent of pet sitters still use traditional methods (telephone or fax) to conduct business, while 32 percent conduct business mostly online and 5 percent use both.

- 84 percent have not incurred any problems using e-mail notifications for employees or clients. Of the 16 percent who did find this method to be problematic, the most common problems were spam blockers and missed e-mails. Other difficulties mentioned included server problems and confusing e-mail messages.

- The number one advantage of having a business web site is that brochures and printed materials used for advertising or marketing are replaced by online information. Professional image and 24/7 communication capabilities

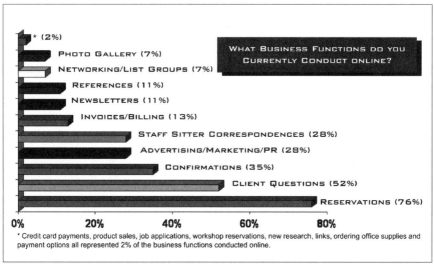

* (2%)
PHOTO GALLERY (7%)
NETWORKING/LIST GROUPS (7%)
REFERENCES (11%)
NEWSLETTERS (11%)
INVOICES/BILLING (13%)
STAFF SITTER CORRESPONDENCES (28%)
ADVERTISING/MARKETING/PR (28%)
CONFIRMATIONS (35%)
CLIENT QUESTIONS (52%)
RESERVATIONS (76%)

WHAT BUSINESS FUNCTIONS DO YOU CURRENTLY CONDUCT ONLINE?

0%   20%   40%   60%   80%

* Credit card payments, product sales, job applications, workshop reservations, new research, links, ordering office supplies and payment options all represented 2% of the business functions conducted online.

Courtesy of Pet Sitters International

tied for second, followed by convenience to pet owners, cost savings, access to hi-tech clients, the site being a sales tool, easy way to conduct business, visibility, and growth.

● The number one disadvantage of having a business web site was that the site must be updated. The second was that web sites are impersonal and you lose the advantage of face-to-face contact. The third biggest was that web sites are time consuming. Additional responses included competition from other sites, prank e-mails, not reaching people who don't have Internet access, cost, creating more business than the sitter can handle, and no opportunity for follow-up or to sell your service.

● 91 percent of those polled said they use a computer to run their business for things like accounting or client databases. The preferred software program was primarily Quickbooks, followed by Microsoft Excel and a variety of other programs.

CUSTOMER CARD SYSTEM

Whether you work alone or you have a dozen pet sitters working with you, you'll need an organized system to run your office efficiently. The customer card system may seem simple, but it works. This is the system I developed and used successfully for ten years in my office. You may want to expand or improve upon it, but it will provide a way of getting started.

Customer Name:	Sitter's Name
Address:	
City, State, Zip Code:	
Home Phone Number:	
Work Phone Number:	
Type of Pet(s):	Price:
Visits Requested Per Day:	
Dates of Services:	
How Did You Hear About Our Service?	

First, the index cards and storage box mentioned in chapter 2 make up your customer card box. When you receive calls for pet-sitting services, you'll need to make a customer card for each client. The sample shown above has some of the pertinent information you should gather when the reservation is made. Write this data in pencil to allow for any necessary changes. You'll find that last names, addresses, phone numbers, and even pets do change.

After you've checked the schedules and assigned a pet sitter to the job, notify the customer who their pet sitter will be (pending a mutually satisfactory initial meeting between the pet sitter and client) and pencil in the sitter's name in the upper right corner of the card. Place the card in a stack of "jobs to notify sitters about" by the telephone.

Sitter Schedule Sheets

After promptly contacting the appropriate sitter for each job, turn to your sitter schedule sheets. A schedule is made for each sitter using your five-column accounting pad. The sample on page 51 shows how I suggest you label your assignment sheets. Only after you've given the sitter information about the upcoming assignment do you fill in the customer's name and dates of the assignment on the sheet. This is your way of making sure you've assigned it. Then place the customer card in a designated space for pending jobs, sorted by the month and week in which they occur.

Having an assignment sheet for each sitter enables you to see at a glance how many jobs each one has and guards against overbooking a person. You'll also need to fill in any vacation time or other dates the sitter is unavailable on each sheet

Sitter Schedule Sheet

Sitter's Name,
Address, and Phone Number
Areas of Service Route

Customer Name	Dates of Service	Job Completed	Payment Received	Sitter Paid	New* Customer?
K. Smith	7/1/06 7/7/06	✓	7/10/06 54.00	✓8/1/06	★

Vacation of Sitter 8/8/06   8/15/06
12/10/06   12/12/06

to help you in assigning jobs. If a sitter has requested assignments only for cats or specializes in birds or the care of exotics, you can note this information at the top of that sitter's schedule sheet. The information will help you, or your office manager, in making the best match for each client's pet-care needs.

Yes, you can keep and track these sitter schedule sheets on a spreadsheet in your computer. I found I preferred to have the sitters' "month at a glance" sheets in front of me on my desk for quick reference as I talked with customers by phone and took reservations.

Checking the Cards

The next step is to check customer cards daily in the ongoing/pending stacks to see which jobs have ended. Place these cards vertically and alphabetically in your customer card box. This tells you the jobs are finished but not yet paid for. By keeping the customer cards turned vertically until payment is

---

Tip

If you're treating your pet sitters as independent contractors, your business and accounting procedures will need to be structured differently to meet the guidelines set forth by the Internal Revenue Service (see chapter 2). A knowledgeable accountant can explain the advantages and disadvantages of using independent contractors for assignments and how to do your record keeping if this is the staffing method you choose.

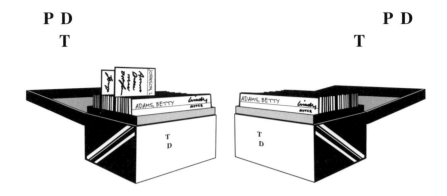

received, it's easy to do a weekly check to see if any accounts are becoming delinquent.

As payments arrive in the office, record the date and amount of payment, then turn the card horizontally in the customer card box. Next, write the date and amount paid by the customer on the sitter's schedule sheet. After endorsing the checks, make your bank deposit. When it's time to write payroll or commission checks, you'll use the "payment received" column on the sitter schedule sheets.

Always write the date the customer's check was received in this column. By referring to this column each month, you can easily see for which jobs the sitter is due payment. Write the date the sitter was compensated in the "sitter paid" column.

And this, in a nutshell, is the system I used in my pet-sitting service. Easy enough, right? The flow chart on page 53 will clarify the steps even further.

POLICIES AND PROCEDURES

Every business has established policies, and your pet-sitting service should be no exception. As a business owner, there are going to be decisions you will have to make regarding the way your business operates. Just as you'll need to determine what your payment policy is (within five days after client returns, thirty days from a contract's starting or ending date, and so on), there are many other issues you will have to determine. Some of these you can decide in advance, while others may surface as time goes by.

My recommendation is that you put your company policies and operating procedures in writing. When a client asks why you don't make pet-sitting visits at midnight, you can honestly explain that it's company policy to finish all pet care rounds before 8:30 p.m. (or whatever time you choose) due to concerns about sitter safety. You can be sure all clients are quoted the same policies, so no

O   P   F

```
┌─────────────────────────────────────────┐
│   Call received. Fill out customer card. │
└─────────────────────────────────────────┘
                    │
┌─────────────────────────────────────────┐
│  Contact appropriate pet sitter for job. │
└─────────────────────────────────────────┘
                    │
┌─────────────────────────────────────────┐
│         Enter assignment on sitter       │
│              schedule sheets.            │
└─────────────────────────────────────────┘
                    │
┌─────────────────────────────────────────┐
│       Place customer card in pending     │
│                jobs stack.               │
└─────────────────────────────────────────┘
                    │
┌─────────────────────────────────────────┐
│      Check pending job cards daily to    │
│    determine completed assignments.      │
└─────────────────────────────────────────┘
                    │
┌─────────────────────────────────────────┐
│      Place finished job cards on side in │
│  alphabetical order in customer card box.│
└─────────────────────────────────────────┘
                    │
┌─────────────────────────────────────────┐
│        Check job finished column on      │
│     appropriate sitter schedule sheet.   │
└─────────────────────────────────────────┘
                    │
┌─────────────────────────────────────────┐
│         When payment received for        │
│             completed job . . .          │
└─────────────────────────────────────────┘
```

| Turn customer card down in customer card box. | Write amount received and date received on appropriate sitter schedule sheet. |

Weekly/Monthly pay sitter for completed assignments. Enter date paid on sitter schedule sheet for each assignment compensated.

one ends up asking you, "Last year you told Mrs. Smith there would be no charge for a visit on Christmas day, so why are you charging me extra?" A policy and procedures manual will also be informative if you hire an office manager or pet sitters to assist you. Having written policies and procedures to refer to will help employees learn about your company and what is expected of them.

Things you should consider when setting policies and efficient operating procedures include:

● **Payment policy:** Will you require deposits? How long will clients have to pay their bills? Will you charge interest on late accounts or fees for returned checks? Will you accept credit cards?

● **Pet-sitting visit hours:** Will you make pet-care visits at any time requested by the customer, or will you make them only within certain time parameters?

● **Office hours:** When can clients expect to reach someone at your business phone or expect to have their call returned?

● **Pet immunizations:** What is your policy regarding immunizations you'll require of pets under your care?

● **House key maintenance and returns:** How will you maintain the security of house keys in your possession? Will you charge extra to personally pick up or return a house key?

● **Initial client interviews:** Will you charge clients for initial introductory interviews? How long will you typically spend, or expect your staff to spend, conducting an initial interview?

● **Job sharing:** Will only one sitter be assigned to each client or will one sitter do morning rounds while another sitter makes the evening rounds? Will you accept assignments where a neighbor or family member is asked to provide some of the pet care during the owner's absence?

● **Leash walking:** Will you require that all dogs you are asked to walk be kept on a leash?

● **Pet identification:** Will your policy be that all dogs and cats under your care wear some form of identification?

● **Last-minute reservations:** Will you accept them if it means you won't have the opportunity to do an in-home consultation with the client and pet? Will you charge extra for last-minute reservations?

● **Holiday surcharges:** Will you charge extra for visits made on major holidays?

This is by no means a complete list of policies and procedures to be considered in a pet-sitting business. However, it is an excellent starting point that I hope will get you headed in the right direction. As I have already stated, there isn't any one way to run a pet-sitting service—although some ways are better than others! I suggest that as you read this book, you make notes along the way of circumstances where it would be smart to have a written policy. And don't forget, policies can always be changed. What works for you in the beginning may need some revision as you and your service learn and grow.

CREDIT CARDS

As small business owners and new business owners, it is sometimes difficult and expensive to get approval to accept credit cards. Not only is there a charge per transaction from Visa, MasterCard, American Express, and all the others, but there are also set-up fees and deposits for the necessary equipment. So in the past most pet sitters requested payment by check or cash.

This practice has started to change, though, as consumers have become more accustomed to using their debit or credit cards for purchases. While there are costs involved for the business owner, accepting plastic does mean that you often get paid faster, and some customers view it as a convenience (or necessity!) and a sign of professionalism.

Talk with your bank about the costs associated with offering this payment method and then shop around. As of this writing, PSI works with a company that offers credit card processing to qualifying members.

TELEPHONE TECHNIQUES

The telephone plays a vital role in your business. The majority of your business will be handled over the telephone. Customers call to get information about your business and to book your services. A phone conversation may be the first impression a client gets of your business, so telephone etiquette is extremely important. Your local telephone company may provide you with business phone tips, so ask if it also provides business etiquette advice. Here are some pointers I can share with you:

- Answer your phone quickly—after two rings if possible.

- Identify your company and who's speaking: "XYZ Pet Sitting Service, Jane Smith speaking."

- Speak in a courteous, friendly, confident tone.

- Smile as you speak! You may feel silly at first, but it really is reflected in your tone of voice.

● Provide as much information as possible about your service. Remember that the inquirer called you and wants to understand your services.

● Patiently try to answer all the client's questions. It's only natural for a potential new client to have some reservations about using your service and allowing a stranger into their home.

● Use the phone to obtain as much initial information as possible about an assignment. Fill out your customer card completely during the phone conversation.

● When using an answering machine or voice mail, personalize your message and tell customers when calls will be returned.

● Return customer calls promptly. This goes for you and your sitters. The sooner, the better!

If you're going to run your pet-sitting service from your home, I have two pieces of telephone advice. First, please have your voice mail or answering machine identify the name of your pet-sitting service when it answers calls. And second, please, please, please, do not allow children to answer your business calls. Nothing takes the "professional" out of a pet sitter faster than hearing a residence answering machine recording or to having a young child babble into the phone.

Telephone skills are extremely important in a service business, so practice and sharpen yours to ensure the success of your pet-sitting venture.

A Sample Narrative

Often, someone will call and say, "I saw your ad in the Yellow Pages and wondered if you could tell me a little about how your service works." You'll need to have a little narrative—a prepared "story" about what your company is and the services you provide. When you have something prepared, you can be sure you have touched on all the important points. Page 57 shows a suggested narrative.

Answering Machines vs. Personal Answering Services

Because pet sitting involves going to your clients' homes, it will be impossible for you to answer your business telephone at all times. But you don't want to miss a call, so you'll need a reliable way for callers to leave you messages. Your most likely options are to buy a dependable answering machine or voice mail system, or to use a personal answering service. There are advantages and disadvantages to both of these methods.

First, a personal answering service gives your business just what the name implies: a personal touch. When you can't be by the phone, your calls are

(For giving out information over the telephone about your services)

Caller: I saw your ad in the Yellow Pages and wondered if you could tell me a little about how your service works.

Pet sitter: What we/I do is provide personalized at-home pet care. We/I actually come to your home so you are able to leave your pet in familiar surroundings. We/I try to follow your pet care routine as closely as possible. This, of course, includes feeding and watering, exercising and giving any medication your pet may require. We/I also spend what we/I call quality time with your pet—just playing, petting and loving so your pet receives personal attention while you're away. We're/I'm happy to keep an eye on your home at the same time by doing such things as bringing in your mail and newspaper, alternating lights, opening and closing curtains and blinds, watering plants—activities that give your home a lived-in look. Our sitters are/I am bonded and insured, and our/my charges are based upon the type of pets you have and the number of visits made. Four days notice is required for our/my services so that we have time to set up an in-home consultation with you and your pet(s). This initial meeting is required before reservations can be confirmed. If you will tell me the type of pets you have and the number of daily visits they will need, I can give you the fee for our/my services.

forwarded to the answering service you've hired. A person answers your calls and takes messages. At your convenience, you simply call the service and receive your messages. Or you may request that the answering service text message your messages to you, if you have that capability on your cell phone.

One problem with this method is that the caller who wants to talk to someone right away may be frustrated by reaching a person who can't do anything more than take a message. The phone operators at an answering service just aren't qualified, authorized, or paid to offer specific information about your services. The other negative is the cost. It is very nice to have calls answered and messages taken by an individual, but there's a price to be paid for this personal service. If there are several answering services in your community, shop around—their prices and services do vary. It's a good idea to check with some of their clients to make sure they are satisfied with the service.

Using voice mail or an answering machine has really become commonplace in recent years. It used to be that everyone hated this technology and refused to leave a message. That's changed dramatically as people have found that with the annoyance of telephone marketers and the busyness of life, telephone answering machines are a fact of life.

When you are considering this tool for your business, find out what type of voice mail services are available from your local telephone company, independently owned communications companies, and computer software packages. I know some pet sitters who installed a computer software program that gives their callers a menu option, such as, "press 1 if you would like information about services; press 2 if you're a client who is returning home; press 3 if you would like to receive a brochure," and so on. This is an impressive setup; however, it may be more sophisticated than you really need if you're pet sitting on a small scale.

One advantage of an answering machine or voice mail system is that it enables you to customize your outgoing greeting messages to fit your immediate business needs. You can record new messages for holidays, seasons, vacation closings, and so on. (You'll find some suggestions for these greetings on page 59.) The biggest disadvantage of an answering machine is probably the fact that it

---

Tip

Because your greeting often creates a first impression of your business, keep it professional. State when callers can expect a return phone call and then meet that expectation. But make your greeting pleasant and interesting, too. If you want to be creative, you can even say something like "leave your message after you hear the bark/meow," or have animal sounds playing in the background as you record your greeting.

Sample Everyday Message
This is XYZ Pet Sitters' answering machine. Our office hours are from
_____ to _____ daily/Monday through Friday (whatever your hours are).
If you need information about our service, please leave your name and
daytime phone number. If you are a client returning home from a trip,
please leave your name and a brief message. Thank you for calling XYZ
Pet Sitters.

Sample Holiday Messages
Happy Holidays! This is XYZ Pet Sitters' answering machine. Our office
hours are from _____ to _____ Monday
through Friday. If you would like information about our service, please
leave your name and phone number
where you can be reached during
these hours. We are rapidly becoming booked for the holidays, so please
make your reservations early to assure
service. Thank you for calling.

Merry Christmas! We're out walking Santa's reindeer now and can't
personally take your call—so we hope you'll talk to our machine. We're
completely booked for the Christmas holidays through December 27.
Our office is closed until 2 P.M. December 28. We still have a few
openings for New Year's and are also taking January reservations at this
time. Please leave your name and number after you hear the beep, and
we'll return your call between 2 and 5 P.M. on the next business day.
Thanks for calling and Happy Holidays.

*Sample   Message   for   Inclement
Weather*
This is XYZ Pet Sitters. Our office is
closed due to the inclement weather.
For those with reservations, sitters will
be making rounds as road conditions
permit safe travel. Messages will be

monitored, so if you have a cancellation, require information or need
to make a reservation, please leave your name and number and we'll
return your call as soon as possible. Begin your message after you hear
the beep. Thanks for calling.

can malfunction. Electrical surges or lightning may create problems, but fortunately, these events are few and far between.

There is usually little chance of malfunction with a voice mail system, but find out any risks associated with each system when making this important decision for your business. Whichever method you choose, be sure that calls are professionally answered and promptly returned.

CELL PHONES

A wonderful invention that I highly recommend for professional pet sitters is a cell phone. When you consider how handy they are for conducting business from your car (pet sitters often do a lot of driving), they are worth their weight in gold. They enable you to check messages and return calls promptly—plus they provide extra security. Fortunately, their prices have really come down in recent years and there are now many calling plans from which to choose. You should be able to find one to fit every budget.

Knowing that help is only a phone call away can be reassuring when you're:

- Walking dogs alone in an unfamiliar neighborhood

- Entering empty homes during evening hours

- Having car trouble

- In need of assistance to locate a missing pet

- Dealing with a pet who is having a medical emergency

- Running late for an initial client interview

Many pet sitters tell me they prefer not to give out their cell phone number as their main business phone line, because clients will call it all hours of the day and night. They prefer to use their cell phone on their own terms and are very selective about whom they give the number to. This is something to keep in mind because when you're first starting out, because it can be tempting to give everyone your cell phone number. Take it from experience, though, that maintaining a little privacy can be a good thing down the road!

While not necessary, if your cell phone can take digital pictures, this option can come in handy. If there is some damage in a client's home that you'll want to document for insurance purposes, voilà, your camera is right there! More than likely, though, you'll use the camera feature more for getting photos of those cute pets entrusted to your care.

ANSWERING E-MAIL

If you're going to use e-mail to communicate with customers, business etiquette applies here also. Be sure to check frequently for messages and respond promptly. Most mailboxes can be set up to respond automatically whenever a new message comes in, simply acknowledging the e-mail and promising a personal reply (I recommend that the reply be by phone) within a certain time frame. It's a bit like the outgoing message on your telephone answering machine, and you can use those examples for ideas of what to put in your automatic reply.

Also be aware of how you phrase things and your choice of wording. Clients only receive the written form of your message and can't hear your tone of voice and your inflections, or see your facial expressions. Something you mean as humorous about a client's breed of dog may be interpreted as insulting by them, due to the nature of e-mail. It's always best to call the customer and discuss their needs and situation by phone if there's any question about how an e-mail message may come across.

DETERMINING SERVICE AREAS

An important part of your preplanning involves deciding where you'll provide pet-sitting services in your community. Initially, you may want to start by working alone and within your neighborhood subdivision, apartment building, or condominium complex, or within a five-mile radius of your home. This gives you the opportunity to make sure you enjoy this type of business without incurring the added responsibility of recruiting, training, and managing other sitters. If your goal is to pet sit on a small scale for supplemental income (perhaps you're retired but want to work at your own pace, have another full-time job, or are a stay-at-home parent), these parameters may be ideal for generating the number of clients you're able or willing to accommodate.

However, if you are ready for the challenge of a larger staff and service area and feel the demand for pet sitters exists in your community, go for it! In three years, I went from two sitters (one being me) to thirty.

To start, get an up-to-date map of your city or town (often available from the chamber of commerce, town hall, or real estate offices) and familiarize yourself with it. It is helpful if you are an established member of the community, in which case you are probably familiar with economic boundaries, growth trends, the safer areas, and, of course, shortcuts around town. If you are new to the community, pet sitting provides a great way to learn your way around, plus meet many neighbors and area residents.

There are several ways to decide where you'll provide pet-sitting services. You can split your territories into north, south, east, and west routes; by zip codes or neighborhoods; by subdivisions or condominium complexes; and so on. Keep in mind the travel involved; if your routes are too extended, your profit may be eaten up in gasoline costs. Define which areas you'll cover and then make sure you're adequately staffed to offer services within them. Also, make sure your advertising defines the areas in which you do business. Otherwise you'll waste a lot of time answering calls and having to explain that your service doesn't extend to the caller's neighborhood.

SETTING PRICES

Setting prices can be difficult for the new pet sitter because, unfortunately, there's no magic formula for establishing a price structure for your services. There are some guidelines, though, that will help you as you tackle this important task.

First, do some basic research in your community. Spend some time making brief calls to area boarding kennels, veterinarians, and any other pet-sitting services to see what they charge for taking care of various animals. This will tell you what the going rates are for pet care and also who your competition is. The cost of living in various parts of the country will greatly affect the charges for such services. Make notes on your findings for comparison and future reference.

Second, decide upon the territories involved for each pet sitter's service route and the traveling distance their rounds will entail. If pet sitters will be using personal vehicles, your prices will need to account for gasoline and wear and tear on their vehicles. The simplest way to calculate this is to use the federal government's approved reimbursement per mile, which as of this writing is 40.5 cents per mile. If a sitter is responsible for a five-mile-radius sitting zone, then the sitter may average around ten miles of travel, or $4.05 in gasoline and wear-and-tear costs, each day. This amount needs to be added to your prices on a per-job basis. A pet sitter may be caring for only one home and pet

---

Tip

Conducting this type of price research is standard in many industries. It is different from the "wannabe" pet sitter discussed in chapter 1 who poses as a customer and conducts a conversation or participates in an in-home interview in order to gain operating information from existing pet sitters.

Tip

Another option is to charge separately for gas or transportation costs. I personally find this method complicated and confusing for the client as well as for the pet sitter! However, if a client lives outside your regular service area, you may consider pet sitting for them with the agreement that they pay an additional amount for mileage, based on the government's current approved mileage charge.

---

and still drive five miles to and from the job. Another time, the pet sitter may be stopping to care for five customers' homes and pets along the same five-mile route. But whether it's one stop or five, the same amount of gasoline and wear on the car is involved, and so transportation costs should be factored into your fees. By using the government's price per mile, you have something concrete and substantiated on which to base this cost. If public transportation is used to make service rounds, that cost and the time involved will need to be considered when setting your prices.

Third, time is another important factor to be weighed in establishing your fees. I expected my sitters to spend five to seven minutes getting to a home, a minimum of thirty minutes in the home, and five to seven minutes returning from the assignment or traveling to the next customer's home. This averages out to about forty-five minutes per home visit. The time and price per home visit increase if there's more than one pet involved.

You'll also want to do some calculations to anticipate what the overhead costs of your business will be. After you've gotten estimates on rent, utilities, telephone, cell phone, printed literature, insurance, bonding, advertising, and so on, calculate what you'll need to earn every month to cover these costs and pay a salary to yourself and to any office help you'll need. To enable you to meet these expenses, you will need to factor a flat overhead cost into each fee, as well as a margin of profit. Don't be surprised if you look at this figure and think, "Gee, who would pay that much for pet care?" You have to remember all the expenses that go into this *professional* pet care service you're providing. And you have to believe that you're worth it and be ready to explain to surprised customers that there is more to this business than simply putting out some pet food. Once customers understand the value of your services, price is usually not a deterrent.

Once you've arrived at your fees, see how they compare with the national average for a pet-sitting visit. This information can be obtained by calling an organization like PSI. Knowing that the prices you charge are within the ballpark of most pet-sitting costs will help you feel more comfortable and confident in setting your fees and in explaining them to your clients.

As of this writing, the national average for a pet-sitting visit is close to $15 per visit. Other useful information is that most pet sitters charge by the visit rather than by the day, and most pet sitters charge an additional amount for each extra pet in the home, applying the highest fee applicable and then adding on—for example one dog at $15 plus one cat at $2 plus one rabbit at $1 equals a total pet-sitting visit charge of $18. If these pets are visited twice or three times a day, the fee is multiplied accordingly.

Another general rule is that most pet sitters charge a slightly higher fee for dogs than for cats. This is because it usually takes longer to adequately exercise and walk a dog. Others charge the same fee per visit regardless of what type of animal is in the home.

A shortcut method to setting prices is to survey what your area kennels are charging for overnight stays, and then add $3 to $7, according to your transportation and overhead expenses, for a per-visit fee. If a client only has one pet, a pet sitter will usually be more expensive than a kennel. Keep in mind though, that if it's a multiple-pet household, a pet sitter usually costs less or is comparable to a boarding kennel.

Some pet-sitting services offer a senior citizens' discount (usually 5 or 10 percent) to encourage business from people 55 and older. A few firms offer a 10 percent discount on monthly contracts or assignments involving ten days or more. They consider this discount to be an incentive for pet owners who are taking long trips. One pet sitter I know offers a 10 percent discount to all clients whose cats or dogs have been spayed or neutered. Firmly believing in spaying/neutering as the solution to the pet overpopulation problem, she sees this discount as a way of encouraging the procedure and rewarding those who do it.

Again, pet sitting is a personal and professional service. Don't undersell yourself or the valuable services offered by professional pet sitters. After all, you're making it much easier for a pet owner to leave home with peace of mind. On the other hand, be realistic in setting your prices—don't price yourself out of reach. Although you can go up or down on your prices, setting your fees and sticking to them will create credibility and give you a more professional image, so it's crucial for you to do your homework. Some trial and error may be involved, and your public will quickly let you know if you're too high or too low. Put forth the effort required to be on the mark and competitively priced.

If you find yourself competing with other pet sitters whose prices are lower because they are not insured and bonded, or they don't operate in a professional manner, don't be discouraged or dissuaded about your fees. My experience has shown that quality always wins out and that people get what they pay for.

Tip

Whenever possible, it is best to stick to your established price structure. However, there will be times when you may increase a fee or offer a discount. Occasionally, someone may book your services who lives two doors away or across the street from you or from the assigned sitter. With no gasoline or great distance involved in the job, you may feel a smaller fee is appropriate, or your sitter may request a lower rate for the customer. On the other hand, a customer may have more than what's deemed normal in houseplants (a greenhouse, for example) that will need watering. If what's needed in a home requires more than the average amount of time you have calculated in your fees, then, of course, you'll raise your fees accordingly. However, a litter of kittens that are still feeding from their mother may not require any additional efforts of a pet sitter, so you should not treat them as additional cats in your sitting fees.

Most of your calls will involve routine pets and the typical care that is included in your established fees. Whenever there is a question, I always try to give the customer a minimum and a maximum figure for services. I then allow the sitter to make the final determination about fees after seeing what the job entails.

Unfortunately, there are some people who quickly go into pet sitting without giving it the proper forethought required. They soon find their prices are too low for them to make any money and quickly become disillusioned, and usually don't last too long in the business. When confronted with the client who tells you, "Such and such a service only charges X dollars for a visit," tactfully reply, "Well, they know what they are worth." Just because someone is cheaper doesn't mean they're better!

Holiday Fees

In the past, many of us thought that working on holidays was simply a part of the job. After all, it's not the customer's or pet's fault that the pet needs care every day of the year! Thus, some of us thought that it was not fair to charge extra for visits made on Christmas, Easter, and so on.

A new trend of charging extra for holiday visits is becoming more commonplace within the industry. Just as a plumber or electrician or other professional charges more for a holiday visit, some pet sitters are adding an extra flat fee ($5 to $10) per visit for rounds made on federal holidays. Many firms give the entire surcharge to the assigned pet sitter as a means of compensating them

---

Tip

Holidays are always busy times for professional pet sitters. Therefore, careful planning is a must. The owner of a very large pet-sitting service told me that she sends out a postcard one month before Thanksgiving that states she is holding a holiday reservation for the customer for the next 72 hours. To confirm the reservation, the client must remit a nonrefundable deposit within this 72-hour period. If the early reservation is not confirmed and the client calls later, they will have to take their chances that a pet sitter will be available. This system helps the office manager preplan for holiday staffing needs. Whatever your system for handling these peak periods, just be sure to double-check all reservations with your pet sitters to make sure no pet-sitting visits are overlooked.

---

at a higher rate for working on holidays. Some firms split the additional charge with the sitter involved.

The idea does have merit and the practice does command professional respect for our industry; however, you'll need to decide what your policy will be. I wanted to charge extra for holidays but when I put the question, along with a vote, to my staff sitters, they vetoed it—to my surprise. The consensus was that it unfairly penalizes the client and might put our services out of reach for some regular customers who weren't used to a holiday surcharge. And because most of our customers showered the pet sitters with holiday gifts, goodies, and/or tips, some said they were afraid the clients would stop this practice if holiday fees were increased.

Although I never was able to implement this policy in my business, it is something to carefully consider. Higher pay would certainly make those holiday visits easier when you'd rather be home or celebrating with family and friends!

COMPENSATING SITTERS

When setting the pay rate or commission splits for sitters working for you, keep in mind the overhead costs, along with the profit you want your business to realize. You'll need to be fair, though, in compensating your staff members. Their time, travel, and work are extremely important to your reputation and success. Although the work is usually very enjoyable, few pet lovers can afford to do it for nominal pay. Set a competitive pay scale that motivates sitters to take pride and do a good job as representatives of your company.

When I set fees for my business, one of the things I considered was the minimum hourly wage. I tried to make sure the pet sitter got a reasonable wage for the time, responsibility, risk, and occasional inconvenience involved in pet sitting. You'll want the wage you offer to be high enough so the pet-sitter position appeals to the caliber of person you want working for you.

Some pet-sitting services pay by the assignment and others pay by the hour; some start sitters at what amounts to 40 percent of the total charges, others pay good sitters as much as 60 percent of the fee charged to the client. Although there is no set pay scale, there are rules for when you're hiring pet sitters as employees (typically paid by the hour) or as independent contractors (typically paid on a commission basis or by assignment). Talk with a good accountant for sound advice regarding compensation rates and methods. And make sure that what you pay is enough to attract the kind of dependable and trustworthy pet sitters your business needs.

"ALWAYS READY" SERVICE

One of the highest compliments you can receive as a pet sitter is when a customer asks you to permanently keep a house key on file. This means they are pleased with your service and plan to use you regularly. It is repeat business like this that helps your business become successful.

Not only does being asked to permanently keep a customer's key mean they like and trust you, it also decreases the amount of time you (and your customer) will have to spend picking up and returning house keys. However, there is increased responsibility and liability involved when you permanently keep someone's house keys. You'll want a formal system in place that encourages clients to become regular clients and that enables you to keep the keys organized and secure while in your possession. You'll also want a permission slip signed by the client allowing you to keep their house key in your possession.

The program I developed for my pet-sitting service was called Ready-Key. We promoted it as a convenience to busy clients who often had to travel on a moment's notice for business or as a time-saving program for frequent travelers who didn't want the inconvenience of meeting us for a key exchange. Although we usually required a minimum of four days notice to pet sit, we were often able to accommodate Ready-Key customers on shorter notice because we knew their pets and routines and already had their house keys. It was not uncommon to never see our Ready-Key customers after the initial interview consultation and first pet-sitting assignment. They simply made reservations by telephone, their pet sitter made the requested pet-care visits, and the client either left payment on the kitchen counter for the sitter or mailed it in upon returning home. It was a great arrangement for all concerned!

To sign up for the Ready-Key program, I had forms printed that stated the customer was authorizing my company to keep two house keys on file (one for our office and one in the possession of the assigned sitter) so that pet-care visits could be made with minimal notice. By keeping one key in the office, we could always get into the client's home even if the regular pet sitter was unavailable due to a scheduled vacation, illness, or emergency. (Accidents do happen, so obtaining two sets of house keys is an ethical and sound business practice.) The client was charged a nominal $5 to enroll in the program, which helped cover our program administration expense.

Each enrollment form was then coded with a number that was also attached to the customer's house key. An index card was also used to record the client's name and Ready-Key code number. The enrollment forms were then filed alphabetically by customer name. The index cards were filed in another secure place by code numbers. The coded house keys were kept in a locked key cabinet. Thus, only my office manager and I knew where each of the files was stored. If my office was ever burglarized, it would not be easy to match up house keys with addresses!

Fortunately, a burglary never occurred and our Ready-Key program became very popular with customers. We even received a couple of calls from Ready-Key customers who had locked themselves out of their homes. Calling their pet sitter to let them inside was less expensive than calling a locksmith! (For this service, we usually charged our basic pet-sitting fee for one pet, because taking this time for an "emergency visit" may have prevented us from making another visit. If it was a regular client, the pet sitter could choose to waive the fee as a courtesy. However, most clients locked out of their home were only too happy to pay a fee, plus an appreciative tip!)

When a Ready-Key client terminates service and requests that their house key be returned or destroyed, it's preferable to return it to them, have them sign a receipt, and then let the client do whatever they want with the key. Keep the signed key return receipt on file.

PLANNING FOR DISASTERS

When I first started pet sitting, the worst calamity I could anticipate for my new business was the possibility of snow and ice during the winter months that would make travel hazardous—or impossible. What would I do if I could not safely get to the pets in my care? While running my business, we not only experienced bad snow and ice storms, but we also had a hurricane and a tornado wreak havoc in the community. Both were very unusual weather for our area, and both caused quite a bit of damage and problems in making pet-sitting visits. These experiences showed me the importance of planning for such events. By having a plan in place, you'll be able to stay calm and take appropriate actions for the well-being of your business and the pets in your care.

Because almost every area is susceptible to some type of natural disaster, such as snow, ice, hurricanes, tornadoes, floods, fires, earthquakes, and terrorism, it's best to prepare a written disaster plan for your business. Many pet sitters make this plan a part of their company's policies and procedures manual and share the plan with their customers. This lets the client know the steps your company would take and what to expect from your service if a disaster occurs while their pet is under your care.

Many pet sitters also encourage their customers to have disaster or first-aid kits made up for each of their pets. The kit should include food and water for up to a week, leash, muzzle, extra ID, proof of rabies vaccination, medications the pet may be taking, bowls, crate and bedding, clean-up supplies, and a current photo. This way, if the pet has to be removed from the home due to a threatening forest fire or an approaching hurricane, a quick exit with supplies can be made.

At the very least, make sure you get the name and phone number of a neighbor or someone within walking distance of your client's home who also has a key to the home; then, if fallen trees or hazardous driving conditions make it impossible for you to visit a home, at least you'll know someone to contact who may be able to get to the home to check on the animal(s). This backup procedure would only be used in an extreme emergency, and your client should be made aware of this. In addition, for pet-sitting reservations during months typically known for hurricanes or snowstorms, it's a good idea to request that your customers make similar arrangements with neighbors, letting them know that you would only call in an emergency. Or, in the case of a hurricane, the customer may request that the pet(s) be evacuated and taken to a kennel or veterinarian's office for safekeeping.

Put some thought and research into preplanning for disasters now. Talk with local professionals and contact such organizations as Emergency Animal Rescue Services (EARS), American Society for the Prevention of Cruelty to Animals (ASPCA), Humane Society of the United States (HSUS), and Noah's Wish for information they provide on disaster preparedness for animals. If you do not have transportation for ice or snow days, find out if your local humane society has a volunteer with a four-wheel-drive vehicle who would assist you or your pet sitters in getting to homes during a snowstorm. Compile your findings into a formal written plan for your business operations during times of disaster. You'll be glad that you have such a reference available—and your clients will be impressed that you have a plan in place!

INITIAL CLIENT INTERVIEWS

The purpose of an initial client interview is twofold. You want the client to have the opportunity to meet you, or the assigned pet sitter, so that they will feel more comfortable with the person to whom they may be entrusting the care of their pet and their home. You (or your sitter) also need this time to get acquainted with the pet and to have the customer personally show you the pet's routine and the household layout. A professional pet sitter should always insist upon this initial meeting before accepting an assignment. You should also let the client know that the reservation is not guaranteed until this introductory meeting has taken place and the client and the pet sitter have signed a service contract.

Here are a few tips for conducting client interviews:

- Allow thirty to forty-five minutes for each interview.

- Remember that first impressions are important. Keep a change of clothes or an extra shirt in your car if you'll be conducting an interview after or in between pet-sitting visits, where you might get covered with pet hair or muddy paw prints. A quick comb or brush through your hair is advisable if you've been outside walking dogs. Although you don't want to wear a business suit to an interview, neither do you want to look like something the dog dragged in.

- Client interviews are business calls, not social hours. Be friendly, courteous, and professional as you lead the meeting. Try to conduct it at a dining room or kitchen table rather than leisurely sitting on a living room sofa. Politely decline any offers for a cup of coffee or snack—especially if you're on a tight schedule!

- The client will be watching to see how you interact and react to their pet(s). Give the pet time to get used to you before making friendly overtures.

- Obtain good written instructions and notes about the care of the pet(s) and home.

- Be knowledgeable and prepared to discuss any company policies, such as payments, late-night visits, insurance carrier, and so on.

The Client Presentation Book

If all goes well and a service contract is filled out and signed, assure the customer that they are in good hands and that you look forward to working with their animal(s). Many pet sitters use what is known as a Client Presentation

> ### Tip
>
> Sometimes family emergencies make it impossible for initial client inter-
> views to take place (for example, the pet owner must leave immediately
> because the death of a relative is imminent). However, be cautious when
> accepting assignments when you haven't met the pet (or client) in
> advance. Get as much information as you can by phone and emphasize
> to the customer that this is an exception to your normal operating pro-
> cedure. I did find that the customers with emergencies whom I was able
> to help on short notice were extremely appreciative and often became
> repeat customers.

Book in conducting initial customer interviews. The Client Presentation Book
is a loose-leaf notebook or scrapbook in which they've included the following
items:

- Business brochure and/or business card

- Copy of their city/county business license

- Copies of any credentials, such as education diplomas or accreditation
certificates, memberships in trade organizations, chamber of commerce, Better
Business Bureau, etc.

- Certificate of liability insurance and dishonesty bond

- Photos of your own pet(s)

- References from pet-sitting customers

- Photos of other clients' pets

- Sample of your service contract

- Business cards from pet sitters around the country or from local pet-
sitting networks (clients are impressed at the size and professionalism of our
industry and are reassured by the camaraderie and networking that often
takes place among pet sitters; get business cards from other pet sitters at local
meetings or national conventions)

The Client Presentation Book enables you to make a professional presentation of your pet-sitting service that is impressive to the customer. It also helps
you lead the interview and keep it on track. If the relationship is determined to

be a good one between the pet, pet sitter, and client, then a service contract can be completed and house key exchanged before the initial meeting concludes.

Some pet sitters charge for this initial meeting just as they would for a pet-sitting visit and others charge but apply the fee toward the first contract if services are used. Others, like myself, don't charge because we see the initial interview as being as much for our own benefit as for the customers'. We prefer to think of the time spent as an initial investment in the future of our businesses. There is no right or wrong way here; it is a decision that you'll have to make for your pet-sitting service.

HANDLING CUSTOMER COMPLAINTS

If you have done a good job recruiting pet sitters and tracking their performance with rating forms or telephone follow-ups, you should have few, if any, complaints. Regardless of how terrific your service is, however, sooner or later you're bound to run into a customer who lives to complain. Or perhaps there will be a legitimate problem and the customer will be justified in criticizing your service or pet sitter. To help you manage such confrontations, I have outlined the way I handled the few complaints that were lodged against my pet-sitting business.

● I always listened with an open-mind to what the customer had to say. Believing in the people who worked for my organization, I conveyed to the customer my surprise and concern about the complaint.

● I next expressed my sincere regret about the complaint and asked for the opportunity to discuss the problem with the pet sitter involved, believing that there are two sides to every story.

● I assured the client I would be back in touch with them promptly and thanked the client for bringing this concern to my attention.

● I then reached the sitter involved as quickly as possible and attempted to get to the bottom of the complaint. If, after hearing both sides of the story, I thought the sitter was in error, I apologized profusely to the client and waived or reduced payment for services rendered. In two situations, I contacted our insurance company to file a claim for the damages incurred by the client (and was thankful I had good insurance in place!).

● If I thought the complaint was not justified, I explained to the client the sitter's and my business's stand or defense in the matter, and that I hoped they understood our viewpoint or action. When appropriate, I had the pet sitter discuss the situation with the disgruntled customer for resolution.

Tip

It's important to have your pet sitters make you aware of any problems they encounter on a sitting assignment. This way, you'll be better informed and better able to address a complaint. Better still is for you or your sitter to call the customer and explain a situation before it becomes a complaint. The daily notes to a client left by a sitter are also used in explaining problems and how they were handled, which can prevent a complaint. When discussing problems, I believe honesty is always the best policy.

I also came to realize that there are some people you can never please and that we were better off without their business. Fortunately, I found these people to be few and far between.

Knowing your sitters helps in these instances. You probably won't know most of your customers, but if you have spent time interviewing and screening your pet sitters, you'll be more confident in believing, trusting, and defending their actions. In addition, keep written evaluations from your clients on each pet sitter to help you feel good about (and be able to defend, as necessary) the people working on your behalf. It's extremely important to recruit and use only those individuals who will be assets to your business. Excellent pet sitters are the key to having no complaints and to the success of your service.

HANDLING DELINQUENT ACCOUNTS

My experience has shown that delinquent accounts are not much of a problem; 99.9 percent of my customers promptly paid their bills after using our services. I like to think that our excellent collection record is a reflection of the quality of our service. Perhaps clients were so pleased that they immediately paid their bills to stay on our good side.

I've also come to believe over the years that people who love their pets enough to hire a pet sitter are not the kind of people who write bad checks or ignore their financial obligations. The occasional straggler I had was usually a client who traveled so frequently that they had simply not been home long enough to sit down and pay all the bills. The stragglers, though, almost always came through and usually included a nice tip as an apology for their lateness. Sometimes it pays to be flexible with your payment terms for unusual situations.

If more than an acceptable amount of time for payment has passed, you may want to call the customer or mail out a friendly past-due letter. You'll find samples of such letters below and on page 75.

To protect myself against late or nonpaying customers, I included a clause in our service contract that specified when payment was due and noted that a monthly interest rate would be charged on accounts unpaid for more than thirty days. I also stated that a penalty would be charged on any checks returned from the bank. Perhaps I was lucky, but I had very few checks returned from the bank for insufficient funds. After I notified the clients, they immediately made the checks good.

Some pet sitters require full payment in advance, especially from new clients. Although this idea has merit and may be more of a necessity in large metropolitan areas, I never instituted the practice in my business. It's my belief that pet owners should be able to use the service, make sure they are pleased, and then pay their bill in a timely manner. I always tried to put myself in the

XYZ Pet Sitters, Inc.

In-Home Pet Sitting Service

Dear Client:

A review of our records indicates a delinquent balance on your account of $_____. This amount is due for our pet-sitting services provided by Molly Smith, from July 7 through July 14, 20__. We hope this has simply been an oversight on your part. We enjoyed caring for your pets and would like to continue sitting for you in the future. Therefore, we thank you in advance for remitting payment to us within the next five (5) days.

Very truly yours,
XYZ Pet Sitters, Inc.

Member of

Bonded
Insured

123 Any Street • Anywhere, U.S.A. 20002
(909) 999-8877 • www.yourwebsite.com

XYZ Pet Sitters, Inc.

In-Home Pet Sitting Service

Dear (Client's Name):

A review of our records shows that you owe a balance of $___
_____ for XYZ Pet Sitters, Inc., services rendered _____
through _____. We believe there are two sides to every
story, so if you'll be so kind as to listen to our side, we'll listen
to your side.

Our Side	Your Side
We provided XYZ Pet Sitter services which you requested in a reliable, trustworthy and caring manner. Our service contract plainly states that payment is due within 3 days after a customer returns from a trip. We regret that in an effort to reduce our overhead costs and keep our service affordable, we are not able to extend credit.	
If you were pleased with our services, we shall appreciate your prompt remittance of fees owed. If you were not pleased, we shall appreciate hearing your side in the right-hand column of this page.	
We appreciate your cooperation and hope that you've just forgotten about your balance owed. We look forward to your continued business.	

Very truly yours,
XYZ Pet Sitters, Inc.

Bonded
Insured

123 Any Street • Anywhere, U.S.A. 20002
(909) 999-8877 • www.yourwebsite.com

Member of
PSI
Pet Sitters
International

customer's shoes, and there was something disconcerting to me about being required to pay in advance for something with which I might not be happy. New clients, in particular, may feel uneasy about upfront payment. However, once clients try your service and are pleased, don't be surprised to find that they leave advance payment for you on the kitchen counter for subsequent home visits.

The only situations in which I did require any advance payment were lengthy assignments that exceeded a certain dollar amount. When this was the case, I insisted that half of the bill be paid up front. My reasoning here is that the longer the assignment, the greater the chance for extra expense: more food or supplies may be needed; the pet may become ill and require veterinary care; or something could go wrong at the home, requiring the services of a plumber or electrician. If any of these things happened, I would have money from the client with which to cover those costs without dipping into the company's bank account. Any additional money owed by the client was then paid upon the client's return. It's not unreasonable to require a deposit on lengthy assignments. However, it is your business, so you'll need to set your own payment policy and be sure it is one you can live with.

Small Claims Court

If you have any problem or dispute in collecting payment from a client, remember that you do have the recourse of small claims court. In small claims court, a magistrate hears cases in which the amount involved doesn't exceed a certain figure, such as $1,500. The specific amount varies by state.

Sometimes just threatening to take the client to court is enough to secure payment. But, if necessary, don't hesitate to use the recourse of small claims court. Taking someone who owes you money to small claims court is a simple, straightforward process, and is relatively inexpensive. The only inconvenience may be the time required to sit in court until your case can be presented. So, if you believe in the job you did for the client and have exhausted other civil means of collecting the payment rightfully due you, by all means, take the client to court.

Being a person of principle, I did use small claims court a couple of times during the ten years I operated my pet-sitting business. The first time involved a client who had contracted with us for a lengthy sitting assignment during the Christmas and New Year's holiday period. The job involved caring for a large dog who was to be visited twice every day, morning and evening.

As fate would have it, our weather turned bad for a few days during this period and we experienced some ice and snow that made travel hazardous. Still, my pet sitter assigned to the job risked the hazardous travel to fulfill every visit as contracted. When the client returned home, he called our office ranting and raving that his dog had destroyed his back door by chewing and scratching. He insisted that this damage was the fault of our service. Not only did he refuse to pay his bill of more than $200, he also insisted that we replace his back door to the tune of $500.

I discussed the situation with the pet sitter, and she confirmed that she had noticed some scratches on the back door but thought they had been there before her assignment began. She also said the dog was very energetic, so such mischievousness was not out of the question for a large breed confined to inside quarters. Damages from pets is a risk that all pet owners face. Since my service did not provide, or contract to provide, 24-hour-a-day care where the pet would be watched every minute, I thought the client was unfair in assigning liability to us and refusing to pay his bill. So I filed a claim for the money he owed us in small claims court. He countered with a claim asking for money to buy a new back door, and to court we went.

Yes, I was nervous and had no idea what to expect, yet I firmly believed we were being unjustly accused of something that was not our fault. After all, a female dog in heat could have crossed the backyard and caused our client's dog to try to tear the back door down. Or someone could have tried to enter the back door (such as an intruder), which caused the dog to go berserk. And because the client was later in returning than anticipated, any damages he was trying to find us liable for could have occurred between the time we made our last visit (termination of contract) and his arrival home. There were just too many variables. Fortunately, after hearing both sides, the magistrate ruled in our favor, telling the client to pay his bill and also our court costs associated with filing the claim.

When an award is made in small claims court, a lien is filed against the person found to be at fault. When this judgment is paid, the lien is removed from the person's record, showing that the debt has been satisfied. In my case, the client paid the pet-sitting bill but failed to pay the court costs, so the lien stayed on his record. Five years later, the client wanted to sell his house. A buyer was found but before the transaction occurred, court records were checked to make sure no liens were held against the home. Guess what showed up? A debt of $29 that was still owed to my pet-sitting service! The client could not sell his house until this was paid and the lien was removed.

More Account Collection Tips

At a pet-sitting convention I recently attended, delinquent accounts were discussed and other pet sitters suggested the following collection methods:

● If you have to send a second delinquent account letter, mail it certified to the customer. The client will then have to sign for the letter, which makes it seem to be of greater importance.

● Show up on the client's doorstep and explain that because you were in the neighborhood, you decided to drop by and pick up the payment due you.

● Ask your 300-pound cousin, Vinny, to stop by and collect the payment.

Do not keep a client's house key "hostage" until a bill is paid, unless your service contract signed by the client states that this is your company's policy. But before making this practice a policy, be sure to check with your attorney for advice about your jurisdiction's applicable laws to make sure such a contractual provision is legal and what steps to take to make sure it is enforceable. And for any house keys that you permanently keep in your possession for happily paying repeat customers, be sure to have a signed document that gives you permission to retain their keys (see "'Always Ready' Service" in this chapter).

Chapter 4

Personnel Choices

Many people intentionally keep their pet-sitting business small, with themselves as the only employee. This enables them to have total control of the services offered, their reputation, and all the fun of pet sitting! While you can't make as much money being the sole pet sitter (there are only so many visits you can adequately make in a day), you can earn some nice income and provide an exclusive, personalized service.

If this is the way you choose to run your business, just make sure you have a backup to cover for you in case you get sick or have an emergency, and that you allow yourself time off from the business. Otherwise, it's easy for a sole proprietor to spread themself too thin and risk burnout.

What often happens, though, is that someone starts a pet-sitting service as a sole proprietor and then becomes so in demand that they are forced to decide whether to increase their staff or scale back on their pet sitting to maintain their sanity. This can be a very tough decision to make, because expanding the business changes your role in it from sole employee to employer. This has been a scary point for many pet sitters, because we tend to think no one can do as good a job in representing our business as we can. How do we ever let go and trust that staff members will do the job the way we want them to?

The good news is that people can be found to work to your standards, and the even better news is that you have a choice in pet sitting with how big you allow your business to be. *You* control your business, and this is something you have to remember from the outset. But whether you choose to start as a sole proprietor or as a staffed pet-sitting service, this chapter contains information every pet sitter needs to know—and also helps you understand how to find good employees, if that's the route you choose.

FINDING QUALIFIED PET SITTERS

The most critical factor to the success of any service business is the people providing the service. You know your own abilities and that you will do a wonderful job of pet sitting, but you have to be absolutely certain you find the right people to help you. There is much at stake in this business of caring for other people's pets and homes, so recruiting personnel is an area that requires careful thought and consideration.

What do you look for in potential pet sitters? My experience has shown they need to be:

- True pet lovers

- Dependable and reliable

- Trustworthy individuals

- Able to provide their own transportation and telephone

- Comfortable and happy meeting the public

With these criteria in mind, you might try approaching your friends, family, and neighbors to ask if they can think of anyone to recruit. Chances are one of them will volunteer to help and you will have your first employee. Be sure to explain, however, that this will be a business relationship with no special privileges.

Other excellent sources of pet sitters are local dog clubs, cat clubs, humane societies, and rescue organizations. Possibly some of their members will be interested in pet sitting or will know of others who would be good candidates. Either call or write to these groups, explaining what your business is and your need for additional pet sitters. On page 81 you'll find the letter I used for this purpose.

Another good way to find qualified staff members is to check veterinarians' offices, especially those located within the area in which you need additional help. Often veterinary technicians or office workers will be interested in pet sitting as a second source of income. With their veterinary hospital experience and an employer's recommendation, these people will most likely be good pet sitters.

Your clients can also be an excellent source of pet sitters. I've obtained some of my best sitters this way. They used our service, were extremely pleased, and then called to see if we had job openings. I had such good luck with clients who became pet sitters that, whenever we needed additional sitters, I advertised in our client newsletter, and I kept an ongoing list of customers who indicated their interest in pet sitting if an opening became available.

XYZ Pet Sitters, Inc.

In-Home Pet Sitting Service

Dear Humane Society Members:

Enclosed you will find information explaining our new pet-sitting business, XYZ Pet Sitters, Inc. Our service is available to pet owners in the city and the surrounding areas. We would appreciate it if you would announce our service at your next meeting.

We also wish to support your organization. Please send us information regarding membership at your earliest convenience.

Our service area covers a large territory and as our business grows, we plan to enroll the services of many more sitters. If your organization has anyone or knows anyone interested in working in their neighborhood area to care for pets, we would appreciate your referring them to us.

We thank you for your time and look forward to serving you and your pets in the near future!

Sincerely,
XYZ Pet Sitters

Member of

Bonded
Insured

123 Any Street • Anywhere, U.S.A. 20002
(909) 999-8877 • www.yourwebsite.com

If possible, try to find sitters who come highly recommended by someone whose opinion you trust. If you do not know the applicants personally, learn as much about them as you can.

When you've exhausted your sources of personal referrals, you may find that you'll need to advertise in your local newspaper under "Help Wanted." I remember being very uneasy at first about using this method. Fortunately, my worries were unfounded, and some very nice individuals applied for our openings. Of course, there were a few less-than-desirable applicants, but I found my instincts useful in weeding these people out. I knew the type of person I was looking for to represent my business, and I could tell almost immediately if a candidate held promise. With time and practice, you'll develop these skills as well. On page 82 you'll find some samples of ads I used in recruiting employees.

Screening Applicants

I know of a few business owners who require each person who answers a newspaper ad to submit a resume. The rationale here is that if the person is professional and interested enough in the job, they will be glad to mail their

credentials to you. If the person isn't willing to meet this request, they are
immediately disqualified. This is a good way to distinguish the good candidates
from the bad, and saves you interviewing time.

Regardless of how you find your pet sitters and how well you know them,
always have job seekers complete an application form. It is best if they return
forms to you directly so you can discuss the position with them. Review applications while the applicant is there to answer any questions you may have and
to get better acquainted. If, after their initial interviews, you feel they are well
suited to be pet sitters, your next step is to check references thoroughly.

I always required at least two personal and two business letters of reference
before permitting any candidates to join my company as pet sitters. (No matter how well I knew them, policy is policy, and it's best to allow no exceptions
to the rule.)

You should also discuss screening applicants with the insurance agent who
sells you your bond. Through experience with bonds, they may have required
applications or suggestions to help you find trustworthy individuals for your
organization.

Some owners of pet-sitting businesses conduct a very thorough investigation of each potential pet sitter. Besides the personal and business references,
they check the applicant's driving record and credit history, and they ascertain
that the applicant has no criminal record. Some business owners look these
records up themselves, while others require that the applicant produce these

records or hire a data-collection service to conduct the various searches. (Before checking references on an applicant, make sure you have their written permission. Many companies will not release information about a former employee without a signed authorization to do so.)

Regardless of the checking methods you use, make every effort to learn as much about your applicants as possible. Due to the nature of pet sitting and the risks and liability involved, you need to feel very comfortable and confident about the character and abilities of your staff members.

An emerging practice in the industry is to administer a personality test to applicants who pass the initial screening. These professionally designed tools give an indication of a person's work ethic, integrity, honesty, and reliability. While nothing can absolutely guarantee a person's character, it's still smart to take advantage of any resource available that will help give you peace of mind about the

> **Tip**
>
> Many business owners are finding it faster and more thorough to use the services of a background screening company when checking references. These companies can check records in multiple states and submit their findings to you in writing for your records. Check your local Yellow Pages for "Employee Background Checks," or call PSI for recommendations.

pet sitters you're sending into other people's homes. Clients will also feel more confident about using your business services when they know the lengths you go to when expanding your staff. Contact PSI for more details on this screening option.

Another requirement I had of my sitters is that they be at least 21 years old. By this age, people usually have a couple of years of work or college experience that add to their common sense and maturity. Customers seem to have more peace of mind in having an adult look after their pets and home than, for example, a high school student.

Who Are Pet Sitters?

Although it was not intentional, all but seven of more than 100 trained sitters I've worked with over the years were female. I find this interesting. As I mentioned earlier, this trend continues, with approximately 88 percent of PSI's pet-sitting firms owned and operated by women. Perhaps the flexible schedule or the nurturing aspect of pet sitting appeals more to women. There are more and more men getting into the field in recent years though, as the demand for pet sitters and the earning potential is recognized.

I have found that pet sitting appeals to teachers, nurses, and graduate students as an extra source of income with flexible hours. Mothers with children in school love doing midday dog walks. While running my business, I had several married couples, two mother-daughter teams, and sisters who worked for my company. These sitting duos were extremely popular with our clientele. Evidently customers liked the double dose of attention their pets receive from a team visit! I also had several real estate agents come on board as pet sitters. The flexible hours worked well with their schedules and enabled them to earn additional money.

Retirees and senior citizens also make great sitters. In addition to enjoying the pets, many love the activity and public contact that pet sitting provides. Many are affectionately known as Grandma or Gramps to their colleagues and clients. I know of several senior citizens who have built their pet-sitting businesses into manageable businesses that provide nice supplemental income, and they can still fit in a game of golf between morning and early evening pet-sitting visits.

There are lots of great people out there who will do a first-rate job of pet sitting for you, so don't be nervous when it's time to expand your staff and delegate more sitting assignments. It's likely that you'll have more applicants for pet-sitting positions than you have openings.

APPLICANT INTERVIEWS

The personal interview is all-important during the recruitment process. Keep in mind that this person may be going on client interviews for your company. Make a note of the following impressions:

- Was the applicant prompt for your interview?

- Was the applicant appropriately groomed and dressed for your meeting?

- What was the applicant's demeanor during the interview—friendly and interested or nervous and ill at ease?

- Would you feel comfortable opening your door and allowing this person into your home on a first-impression basis only?

During the interview, you'll want to go over the position requirements and get more in-depth answers to questions asked on your application form. If the applicant works another part-time position, find out the hours involved and if they will conflict with your position requirements. Have the applicant elaborate about ownership of pets, present and past. Ask questions to draw out the applicant in conversation. This will help you evaluate his or her speaking skills, intelligence, and personality.

Although I always conducted interviews at my place of business, I know of some pet sitters who prefer to interview at restaurants. They say this enables them to assess the applicant's table manners and comfort level in a public setting—plus it allows them a lunch or dinner as a business expense! Other pet sitters prefer to conduct an initial interview at the applicant's home. This enables them to see, among other things, how tidy the applicant is, along with the type of pet(s) the applicant owns. They think they get to know the applicant better after seeing them on their own turf. Yet other pet sitters insist that the initial interview be held in their own homes. This setting allows them to imagine the applicant as if he or she

> **Tip**
>
> Don't forget professional courtesy once you've found your new pet sitters. It's my opinion that if someone has taken the time to complete an employment application and talk with you, the least you can do is mail a letter of explanation or rejection. Applicants are grateful for the notification, and this attention to detail speaks well for your company.

was making an initial visit to a customer's home. How the applicant interacts with the owner's pets is an important part of the evaluation process!

Become familiar with labor laws so that you are not discriminatory in your hiring practices. Contact the Department of Labor or local office of the Wage and Hour Administration for current laws affecting employers.

SITTER ORIENTATION

Whether it's one new pet sitter or an entire group, it's very important to have an orientation session to train your sitters. You'll want them to understand your company's policies and procedures, and your expectations of them as members of your staff. The more informed your pet sitters are, the better job they'll do as representatives of your company.

Attendance at an orientation session before any new pet sitter takes on any assignments should be mandatory. After this session, many of my pet sitters told me they had no idea so much was involved in being a professional pet sitter. They were amazed and appreciative of all the information conveyed during our training session. They were also surprised at the length of the session: from four to six hours, depending on the number of questions raised and the amount of discussion.

Tip

You may want to require your pet sitter employees to sign a noncompete clause before joining your company. This would prohibit your employees from taking your customers and starting a competing business for a certain period of time after leaving your employment. Discuss this with your attorney—a noncompete form or clause is a legal contract. You'll need legal assistance in preparing a document that will protect you in your state.

To help you conduct your own training sessions, I will give you an overview here of what took place in mine. This is only a suggestion of possible format and content. Depending on your location and climate, there may be some specialized services your company will want to provide (for example, pool cleaning) in addition to the more general services provided by a pet sitter. The basics follow, and you can tailor your own orientation to fit the specifics of your business.

The Basics

I began each session with introductions and then handed out folders of supplies that the pet sitters would use when working (service contracts, business brochures and cards, notepads, key tags, self-addressed envelopes, and so on). I next explained that the purpose of our training session was not to scare new pet sitters with all the things that could go wrong, but instead to prepare them so they could avoid any problems and know how to handle them if they arose. I wanted my sitters to always be thinking and using their common sense.

After presenting some history of our company and the pet-sitting industry itself, I discussed certain company formalities, along with policies and procedures. These included:

- Compensation—when and how much the sitter would be paid

- Our company's insurance coverage

I next showed training videos. The video *Professional Pet Sitting I—The Basics* takes a new sitter step by step through an actual pet-sitting visit. *Professional Pet Sitting—Tips from the Pros* goes beyond the basics with tips for being a successful pet sitter. These videos are great training tools and also enable the presenter to take a break and rest their voice for a little while. (See the appendix for where to buy these videos.)

Points to Stress

During an orientation session, here are some points you should stress to new pet sitters:

• Emphasize the importance of confidentiality of customers' names. You never know who may overhear your conversation as you describe the gorgeous art, coin, or gun collection in the Smiths' home. Customers' names and the contents of their homes should remain absolutely confidential; letting their absence be known could invite a burglary. Coding house keys anonymously is also important in case keys are ever lost or stolen. I instructed my pet sitters to code them by visit or stop (1, 2, 3, and so on). That way, only the pet sitter knew to which house the key belonged. Make your customers aware of their anonymity; this gives them peace of mind while they are away.

• An introductory meeting with the client and their pets is an absolute must, unless extenuating circumstances preclude it. This is normally a thirty- to forty-five-minute visit that gives the client time to fill out your service contract and gives the pet sitter a chance to become acquainted with the pets and their routine. The meeting helps the client feel comfortable because they know the person who will have responsibility for their pet and their home. It also ensures that the pet sitter knows the assignment is one they feel comfortable accepting. Walking into a stranger's home and dealing with a pet you've never met before is an eerie feeling. All in all, an initial interview is highly recommended.

• Returning clients' house keys can be handled in different ways. Some customers prefer the key be left in their home on the final visit. Others want it held by the pet sitter and returned in person, just in case the owner is not able to return when planned. Many people these days have dead-bolt locks for which a key is necessary to lock the door, so the key has to be returned in person. (In such cases, you may want to charge extra for the pet sitter's time and gasoline in returning the key, unless you've already allowed for this when setting your fees.) Many of our regular customers signed up for the Ready-Key program (discussed in chapter 3), and we kept the extra key in the central office. This is nice, as it shows that the client likes your service and also cuts down on time and gasoline for key pickups. In any event, you'll need to inform your new pet sitters of your company's key-return policies.

• Undoubtedly you have put thought and research into setting fees for your pet-sitting services. Thoroughly explain your pricing during orientation and spell out what the customer receives for this fee. Although you or whoever answers your business phone will usually quote prices for services, sitters should understand how to calculate fees and be able to respond intelligently to routine inquiries about prices.

Tip

I know of one pet sitter who stamps her service contracts with "100 per-cent of gratuities go directly to your pet sitter." This not only tells the client that tips are accepted, but it also lets them know that they go directly to the pet sitter. Since implementing this idea, she told me that tips from clients had really increased and, of course, her pet sitters were thrilled!

● Discuss your company's payment policy. Do clients pay their sitter directly and trust that payment will be forwarded to the company, or do clients mail payment to your office? Are major credit cards accepted, and if so, how is this handled? Are sitters allowed to accept tips, and if so, must they report them for proper taxation by your company? And do they keep the entire tip or split it with the company? This is an important area that requires serious attention to avoid any confusion or misunderstanding.

● Speaking of tips, inform new sitters not to be surprised by customers who remember their pet sitter with a souvenir or gift from their travels. Point out how good you feel when you make rounds during holidays and find a Christmas gift or a Valentine's box of candy for you from Muffin or Snowball or Fluffy. These thoughtful little remembrances from customers can make your day.

● Because driving is such an important aspect of pet sitting, stress to your sitters the need for careful driving habits at all times. The last thing you want is a speed demon representing your organization. Also, a clean car speaks well for the integrity of your pet sitters.

Tip

For your own peace of mind, you may want to obtain an umbrella auto-mobile insurance rider for your business. (This coverage was mentioned in chapter 2 under "Insurance," but deserves repeating.) If one of your pet sitters has an automobile accident while pet sitting and expenses exceed the limitations of their car insurance, your business policy would offer additional coverage. Discuss this with your insurance agent.

● Discuss the type of notice you'll expect from pet sitters for vacation, illness, and even resignation. You will need advance warning to reschedule assignments and guarantee services to clients. Requiring a week's notice from sitters is reasonable; sitters usually know of upcoming vacations, appointments, or exams. Of course, you can never plan on the flu, so have a backup plan to cover for sick employees, or you'll find yourself scrambling at the last minute to feed hungry pets.

● Insist that your pet sitters recognize and take advantage of free advertising at every opportunity. Advertising is expensive and sometimes beyond the reach of the small business, yet it's vital to any new business. There are many ways to spread the word about your services, though, with little or no expense. Ask pet sitters to always carry business cards and/or brochures and post them on bulletin boards in public places. Leave these items in a variety of business establishments and hand them out at social and civic gatherings. When shopping, give business cards to salesclerks. Give thought to places and people you may not have considered before; even those who may not have a pet probably know people who do and who may need your services. Word of mouth is often the best form of advertising for a service business, so implore your pet sitters to spread the word about the pet-sitting services your company provides.

● If you have not already mailed a brochure to a new client describing your services, request that your pet sitters leave one during their initial meeting. The fact that you have printed literature creates a more professional image for your business, so take advantage of it.

● Suggest that your sitters study literature from your office library, the public library, or web sites to familiarize themselves with the various types and breeds of dogs, cats, and other household pets. A client will always be impressed when a pet sitter is knowledgeable about their particular pet.

● Tell your pet sitters the name of your insurance company and your agent's name. Discuss with them what your insurance covers, stressing the need for their conscientiousness while pet sitting. I gave each of my sitters a letterhead form, signed by my insurance agent, which briefly explained the types of insurance coverage my business carried. This was proof of our coverage if a customer ever requested it.

● If the information had been available to me, I would have shared reasons that insurance claims had been filed by pet sitters in order to educate my pet sitters not to make these same mistakes! Today's pet sitter is fortunate that our industry does have a claims history to learn from, and I have shared some of the most common or most outlandish of these claims in chapter 7 in "Don't Do This!" Please share these examples with your pet sitters so that you won't find yourself needing to file an insurance claim for the same reasons.

● A true sign of a conscientious, professional pet sitter is a daily note or visit log left in the customer's home. This should state the time of the visit, how the pet sitter found the pets and home upon each visit, weather conditions, and so on. I furnished "daily diaries" for this purpose, but if you do not want to go to this expense, insist that a note be left on company letterhead. Customers have raved about these notes and have said they enjoyed reading them very much. The daily record gave them assurance the pet sitter was there and made them feel as if they hadn't really been away. Some pet sitters are brief in their notations and others write essays on the antics of the pets. The notes come in handy if a customer returns early and wonders if the pet sitter has already fed the pet(s) that day. Also, if a pet acts peculiarly, the pet sitter can make daily notes to cue the owner in to a potential problem. If a problem has occurred, the sitter can explain in the daily note what has transpired. Otherwise, the customer may wonder what took place in their absence. The daily notes are a very important part of your service. If pet sitters are doing a good job, the customer should not be able to tell the sitter has been there—except for the daily note.

● You'll want to know if customers are pleased with your services. A good way to get feedback is to have pet sitters leave some kind of evaluation form. Discuss the importance of this form with your new sitters. You or your pet sitter may also want to provide a self-addressed envelope with the evaluation form to encourage customers to return the form (and their payment!) to you. A rating form gives you valuable information based on customers' comments, suggestions, and even constructive criticism. You can also use it to find out how they heard about your services to assess what form of advertising is working for your business. If pet sitters are to leave a self-addressed envelope for the client, encourage them to provide business-sized envelopes. Clients don't like to fold their checks or forms origami-style to fit in small envelopes!

● Returning customer calls promptly is a must for you and your pet sitters to create a professional, positive image for your business. If it takes three days to return a call, a customer may wonder if your delivery of services is also haphazard. Even if customers are not leaving town for several weeks, they still appreciate speaking with their sitter and knowing they can count on the prompt, professional services of this individual. After talking with their sitter and being assured of services, customers are relieved and feel secure in making flight or travel reservations. So always insist your pet sitters call and introduce themselves to their customers as soon as possible—and preferably within twenty-four hours of the client's call to book pet-sitting services.

● First appearances do make strong impressions, so remind your sitters of this and request that they be neat and clean when going to an initial interview. To project a professional image, pet sitters should not smoke, chew gum, or accept an alcoholic beverage while representing your company. Smoking can plant the fear of a house fire in customers, while accepting an alcoholic beverage can create concerns about raids on their liquor cabinet. So, even though pet sitting is very informal, it is best to forego any of these activities because they reflect negatively on your professional image. Besides, house visits for interviews and service rounds do not take up a lot of time—and all that time should be spent on the business at hand. Insist that your pet sitters refrain from smoking, drinking alcohol, and chewing gum while on duty.

● Suggest that pet sitters establish a designated area within the client's home where last-minute instructions or payments may be left by the client and daily notes, logs, or diaries kept by the pet sitter may be found. A location may be the kitchen counter, dining room table, or under a magnet on the refrigerator door.

● Taking the garbage out on a final visit to a customer's home is a nice touch and speaks well for the thoroughness of your services. Empty cans of pet food in the trash tend to smell as they accumulate. Depositing the trash in an outside container results in a more pleasant return for your customer. If your customer is away for an extended period of time, the pet sitter may need to take the trash out more often.

● Advise new pet sitters never to let a client leave a key hidden outside for them. Clients are notorious for leaving town in a hurry and forgetting this all-important task. An extra key can be made for a very small charge and given to the pet sitter, but a locksmith can be expensive, not to mention the extra time this will entail. Also, don't agree to let clients drop their house keys in the pet sitter's mailbox. Mail carriers have been known to pick up these keys (or envelopes with keys in them) and assume they are to be conveyed through the postal system.

● If a pet sitter learns about the death of a client's pet, they should let your office know. Then you can change your records accordingly and send a sympathy card or remembrance to the customer.

● Remind new pet sitters that feces should always be disposed of in a sanitary manner. Insist that the client or pet sitter provide plastic bags for this phase of cleanup.

● By requiring a certain amount of notice from clients before their departure, you should have ample time to arrange for an initial interview with their assigned pet sitter. However, clients will have emergencies due to illness or death and need to leave immediately, without meeting the pet sitter. Discuss these emergency situations with new pet sitters and your company's policy in handling them.

● Tell pet sitters to always try contacting their absent clients if a disaster occurs in your area. If there is an earthquake, tornado, or hurricane, clients will most likely hear of it through the media and worry about the safety of their home and their pets. The pet sitter should call the client promptly and give as much information as possible.

● If you have developed a formal disaster plan for your service, you should discuss it and recommended operating procedures with new pet sitters. Be sure to copyright it before distributing copies to personnel.

● Spend some time discussing how emergency pet-sitting situations should be handled. Should pet sitters contact you at home, call another staff member, or handle the problem as they see fit? Prepare your new pet sitters with a plan of action for emergencies so they won't panic.

● Get emergency numbers from your new pet sitters. If a staff member becomes sick or injured while pet sitting, you'll need to know whom to notify. And if you can't get in touch with one of your pet sitters, you may need to check with this emergency contact to ascertain their well-being and whereabouts.

● More than likely, the insurance and bond coverage you purchase for your business will only cover your pet sitters while they are in the course of performing pet-sitting duties. Stress to your pet sitters that for this reason, among others, they should always go alone when making pet-sitting rounds. The customer has authorized *only* the pet sitter, as your company's representative, to have access to their home and pets. If an adult friend or family member accompanies the pet sitter and even sits in the car, neighbors may be watching and later exaggerate the scene by describing "a carload of people" who showed up to care for the pets. To avoid any unnecessary problems, the pet sitter should always work alone. If a pet sitter knows there will be a time

when someone may accompany them on a visit, they should ask the client's permission beforehand and get acknowledgment in writing. If a pet sitter requires assistance after the fact with an assignment, you will need to intervene, making the client aware of any problems and the reason additional people were needed to enter their home.

● Furnish pet identification tags that state the name of your company and business phone number. Instruct new pet sitters to place one on each dog or cat who has access to the outdoors for which they will be sitting. If the pet becomes lost (after darting out the front door when the pet sitter is entering!), anyone finding the pet will know whom to call. (See the appendix for ordering information.)

● Distribute Pet Sitter Emergency Notification cards to your pet sitters and ask that they keep these with their identification cards and driver's license. If the pet sitter is in an automobile accident or becomes sick or falls unconscious, this wallet card states that there may be pets under their care who need attention and who should be contacted (most likely the business owner—you!).

● A final word of advice you could offer is to encourage your new pet sitters to conduct business by the Golden Rule. Treating each customer, pet, and home as they would their own will surely minimize the potential for problems and help pave their path to success.

The Equipment List

I remember when I first opened my pet-sitting business, I tried to think of everything I might possibly need in the course of pet sitting. I bought so much—paper towels, garbage bags, pooper scoopers, flashlight, whisk broom, and so on—that I had to carry a huge bag to make rounds. What I quickly learned was that people who have pets have the items necessary to do a good job caring for their pets. The initial items I suggested my pet sitters invest in included the following:

• A clipboard to hold service contracts so the customer has a hard surface to press on when filling one out. While the customer completes the contract during the initial interview, the sitter is free to get acquainted with the pets in the household.

• A key holder of some type is absolutely mandatory, whether it's a string or bracelet around a wrist or a belt clip-on. There is nothing more horrifying than to have the wind blow the door shut (and locked) while the sitter is outside with the pet and the key is on the kitchen counter. This is not only embarrassing, but it can be time-consuming and expensive if a locksmith is required to get the sitter back into the house. So stress to your sitters the importance of keeping house keys attached to their bodies while making pet-sitting rounds. I have tried all types of key holders and found that my pet sitters and I preferred the elasticized plastic wristbands. They are available at most hardware stores.

• A city map is helpful for shortcuts and finding streets when you think you know where you are going—but don't.

• A schedule book, whether it's a date book or simply a monthly calendar, is absolutely necessary for keeping up with pet-sitting visits, initial interview appointments, and staff meetings, not to mention all the other things one may need to remember in this busy day and age. Write everything down so you don't find yourself needing to be in two places at the same time.

- A flashlight can be very useful when pet sitting. It can help you enter a dark home or find an elusive cat who hides in nooks and crannies, and it can serve as a weapon if need be (the battery-filled handle can pack a powerful punch if you ever need to defend yourself with it).

- A leash is a necessity, because although clients should always provide one for walking their dogs, sometimes they forget to leave it where you can find it. Also, a worn leash could break from the strain of an energetic dog. Having a backup leash can prove handy.

- Flea repellent is a necessity for the occasional home that's filled with fleas. You don't want to carry the fleas into the home of another client or back to your own home. Nor do you want to be eaten alive while caring for the household pets. So invest in a good flea repellent.

The Paperwork

The next part of my orientation and training session for pet sitters involved going over the various literature and business forms my service used. These items were placed in the information packets mentioned at the beginning of this chapter. Although some of the forms were self-explanatory, I still reviewed each one. I wanted to make sure new pet sitters understood the reason for each piece of printed material and knew how and when to use it. Because you'll want your new pet sitters to be thoroughly informed, I suggest you devote some time to explaining the forms and literature in your training sessions.

First Aid

Although pet sitters are not expected to be roving veterinarians, a good pet sitter should be able to recognize the symptoms of illness in a pet and have some knowledge of first aid if a pet becomes injured or sick while under your company's care. I know of a few pet-sitting services that require their new pet sitters to volunteer several hours at a local veterinarian's office, thereby gaining valuable experience in dealing with sick or injured animals. The American Red Cross teaches a pet first-aid class, as does Pet Tech. This is valuable training for professional pet sitters, and is usually offered at annual Pet Sitters International conventions.

Another way of approaching first aid in your training sessions is to show videos that deal with the subject. Although these were not available when I first began to expand my staff, there are now a few good ones on the market. There are also interesting videos available on the proper care of rabbits, ferrets, and various types of birds and reptiles, along with cat care and dog breed identification. Most videos and pet books are reasonably priced, so consider providing an office library of first-aid and pet-care books and videos that new sitters may borrow. Given the low cost of some of the books, you might give each new pet sitter a paperback book on general first aid for pets, or you could require that pet sitters purchase a copy as part of their start-up supplies.

The Quiz

After a final question-and-answer period, I concluded my training sessions with a pop quiz. This was a multiple-choice test that included questions from all the areas addressed in our orientation. The test enabled me to see which new pet sitters had a complete understanding of what pet sitting involved and what our company policies and procedures were. By looking at the test scores, I could see which areas needed further clarification or which attendee had slept through the training program. (Anyone napping during the session would have been immediately disqualified from joining our staff; however, I'm glad to say this never happened!)

An additional benefit of the test was that clients were always impressed when they learned that my pet sitters were not only trained, but they were tested as well. Thoroughness in training heightens the level of professionalism and increases credibility. Make every effort to your new pet sitters—and yourself—start on the right track. These initial investments in hiring and training will really pay off in the long run.

SURVIVAL BAG

In addition to the recommended pet-sitting supplies previously discussed, there are a few more items that I, and many of my colleagues, have found to be helpful in the course of pet sitting. Most professional pet sitters purchase a canvas bag or fanny pack that is referred to as the Pet Sitter's Survival Bag. This bag is kept in the car or another convenient place so it can easily be thrown over the shoulder before heading out to make pet-sitting visits.

Items kept in the Survival Bag include paper towels (why are there usually only two left on the roll at a client's home?), rubber gloves, a can opener, a hooded rain slicker (for unexpected downpours), WD-40 (for temperamental house keys; in a pinch, a lead pencil also works pretty well), pet toys, a pet first-aid kit, a human first-aid kit, tissues, snacks, personal grooming items (comb, brush, makeup, and so on), a squirt bottle or water gun filled with water and lemon juice or vinegar (to divert stray dogs who try to approach you when walking a dog), identification, spare change, and poop disposal bags.

Other supplies, such as a clipboard and business literature, can also be carried in this bag. If you come up with other recommended items for "survival" as a professional pet sitter, please write to me at the address included for Pet Sitters International in the appendix. I'd like to share your ideas with readers in future editions of this book.

SITTER SAFETY

Professional pet sitters, like real estate agents and pizza delivery personnel (there's that pizza analogy again!), are at risk because they go into strangers' homes for interviews, enter empty homes during pet-sitting visits, and walk dogs or exercise pets outside at all hours of the day and evening. Thus, pet sitters should not be naive or complacent about personal safety.

Incorporating some discussion of this issue into your orientation session is highly recommended. Stress to your pet sitters that this subject is not meant to scare or deter them from pet sitting, but merely to increase their awareness of an important subject. As the saying goes, an ounce of prevention is worth a pound of cure. The following are some safety tips I've gathered from my years in pet sitting.

● Be alert. If you feel uncomfortable in a situation, get out of it.

● Keep your photograph and those of other pet sitters on file in an easily accessible place in your office. Also keep a list of car models and license numbers, driver's license numbers, whom to contact in case of emergency, and any important medical information. (Consider having each new pet sitter write this information on an index card during orientation and then clip it to a Polaroid picture you take of each sitter before the session ends.)

● Report any suspicious experiences to local law enforcement right away.

● Develop a coded distress signal with your office personnel, pet sitters, and/or your family. This would permit the person in danger to call the office or home with a message that sounds innocent but would alert others that something is wrong and help is needed.

● If you are uncomfortable at an initial meeting with a client, say that a backup sitter (or your spouse) will be showing up at your location any time now, as it is usual company policy for two people to know the location of every customer's home and pets in case of an emergency.

● Dress conservatively for initial interview meetings with customers.

● Don't carry a pocketbook while pet sitting. Instead, keep identification and necessary items on your body in a fanny pack. And leave the jewelry at home!

● Carry a personal alarm or shrill whistle and don't hesitate to make as much noise as possible if you feel threatened. Yelling "fire" or "911" alerts others to an emergency.

● Make sure you know beforehand who else (and what type of car they are driving) has access to the client's home.

● Never allow anyone else (other than those authorized in writing by your customer) into the client's home.

● Familiarize yourself with the areas in which you provide sitting services. Know safe routes for dog walking, the location of police and fire departments, stores and restaurants that are open late, and so on.

● Keep your car in good running condition with your gas tank filled. Remember to lock your car doors while driving and while parked at clients' homes.

● Other than your staff or family members, don't let anyone know absent pet owners' names and travel dates.

● Leave an outside light on (or ask clients to use timers) so that evening pet-care visits don't have to be made in the dark.

● Have house or car keys in hand and ready to use when arriving and departing during your pet-sitting rounds.

● Carry a cell phone with you while pet sitting.

The following are more helpful tips from various pet sitters on the subject of sitter safety. (Thanks to the members of Pet Sitters International who contributed these suggestions for personal safety while pet sitting—you know who you are! Imparting ideas like these helps our industry as a whole and makes membership in a professional organization so beneficial and valuable.)

● Make noise when you enter an empty home. If a burglar is inside, he may run the other way. If the client or a family member is there, they won't be surprised by your appearance.

● The initial client interview should tell you what the animals, customer, and home are like. Don't take the job if you are uncomfortable with any of these!

● Lock the door behind you when entering a client's home.

● Always call the dog's name before entering, and turn down the job if the dog is aggressive or has ever bitten anyone.

● Personalize the home by repositioning an item in the house near the entrance. If you see it's been removed or disturbed, you'll be alerted that undesirable activity may have taken place.

● Advise a friend or family member of when, where, and for how long you're meeting a new customer, along with contact information. Ask them to call your cell phone during the meeting so you can alert them (through a secretly understood code phrase) if you have any concerns about your safety.

● Check with your local police department for any booklets they have available on home and personal security.

● Share pertinent safety tips with customers.

● Do a complete outdoor security check of the house before entering, making sure doors and windows haven't been broken into or tampered with. Be aware of your surroundings, indoors and outdoors. A forced door, broken window, or missing items means you should leave immediately and call the police.

● Ask pet sitters to call and report the time of arrival and departure at each client's home. Call your own answering machine with updates of the time, where you are, and where you're headed for visits.

● Carry mace or pepper spray with you, but make sure you know how to use it. Also, consider taking martial arts or a self-defense class.

● Don't accept jobs in unsafe neighborhoods, and take someone with you for evening visits. (Remember to get prior authorization from the client.)

● Ask someone to accompany you if you ever feel uneasy about making a visit.

● Wear reflectors on your shoes and clothing so cars can see you at night.

● Remember that the dog you're walking can be a warning system. Pay attention if the tail stops wagging or the ears stand up!

● Have a rehearsed plan in your mind so that if you're attacked while walking a dog, you know exactly where your whistle/personal alarm/pepper spray is or what you will start screaming.

● Be familiar with two exits from each client's home.

● Park in well-lighted areas, when possible, and always lock your car doors while making pet-sitting visits.

SITTER NUTRITION

This is a relatively new subject for pet sitting, but one that I think needs addressing because it's something you don't think about when you're first starting out. In the "old days" when I, and pet sitting, were much younger, we never gave a thought to something like sitter nutrition. We were so glad to be working and pet sitting for people that eating—much less eating correctly—was the least of our worries! Now, with the public emphasis on eating healthy, pet sitters have expressed concern at national, regional, and local meetings about how to eat right with the hectic schedules they sometimes face.

With careful planning, you don't have to sacrifice nutrition just because you're often working during normal meal times. Here are some suggestions that are helpful to share with staff members, especially at orientation sessions for new pet sitters.

● Pet sitters are known to frequent fast-food places. If you must, order grilled or sliced meats, not breaded or fried.

● Try a low-fat muffin or bagel for breakfast.

● Order a small hamburger instead of a deluxe or super. Better yet, order a salad.

● Use catsup, mustard, or vinegar instead of mayonnaise.

Keep a cooler in your car and plan ahead for meals or hunger pains by carrying these foods with you:

● Low-fat snack crackers, pretzels, or popcorn

● Fresh fruit

● Homemade soups or stews—in Thermos containers or ask clients for permission to use their microwave oven

● Canned fruit, tuna, or chicken in pop-top cans

● Fruit juices

- Low-fat breakfast bars, fig bars, or drinks

- Veggies—easy to carry in a small cooler

- Graham crackers or low-fat cookies

- Low-fat potato chips or nacho chips

- Dried fruits—raisins, apricots, dates, and so on

- Lots of water

- Protein bars

- Bites of cheese (in a cooler)

- A healthy sandwich

- Containers of cottage cheese or yogurt (in a cooler)

Eating on the run does take planning, but thinking ahead can result in a healthier diet as well as maximum use of time spent in the car at traffic lights or during rush hours. Suggest that your new pet sitters give serious thought to this, because most pet-sitting rounds are made during breakfast, lunch, or dinner hours. Remind them, too, of the calories they will be burning while walking and exercising pets.

MANAGING AND MOTIVATING SITTERS

Starting your own pet-sitting service may present you with your first experience managing employees, and you may need some assistance or reassurance in this area. First, remember that a pet-sitting business is somewhat nontraditional compared to other business environments. After you've recruited and trained your staff members, you'll probably find that you communicate mainly by phone and rarely see them. That's why I feel that pet sitting is one of the few businesses that still thrives on the old-fashioned element of trust. There must be trust between the client and the pet sitter, as there must be trust between the pet sitter and the employer. You won't be able to follow your pet sitters and check on the jobs they do for you; you'll have to trust that they will satisfactorily fulfill their job obligations. You will also need to trust that clients will let you know if they are displeased with your company's services.

That's why it's important to use some type of client evaluation form or to call your clients for feedback about your pet sitters and services. Then share

---

Tip

Because you'll be seeing your staff members infrequently, consider taking or requesting their photos for display on your office bulletin board. This enables you or your office staff to put faces with names and personalizes your operations a little more. You'll also be able to give a physical description of the pet sitter for identification, if requested to do so by a client. And, as discussed in the previous section on safety, this is a wise precaution.

---

this information with your sitters. If they are doing a terrific job, tell them, praise them, commend them! Let them know how much you appreciate their efforts. Likewise, if there's any type of complaint or dissatisfaction, constructively discuss this with the sitter, then put your discussion and the outcome of it in writing and file it in the pet sitter's personnel file. If the same complaint is voiced again about that pet sitter, you'll have good documentation for supporting whatever disciplinary action you decide to take. Hopefully, if you've gone to the trouble of finding good pet sitters, you'll be singing their praises instead of disciplining them.

Pet sitting is different from more traditional businesses in that it usually requires part-time or split-shift employees who work on call, usually with no guaranteed paycheck and minimal benefits, if any. The work can be demanding, with weekends and holidays often the busiest times and, as with any job, you need to be on guard against burnout. Make sure your pet sitters have an occasional weekend or holiday off. Keep enough pet sitters on staff or backups available so that you're not too dependent on any one pet sitter. If you started your pet-sitting business by making all the visits yourself, remember what some of the jobs and some of the clients can be like—and be considerate of your staff members! If you're good to your employees, they'll be good to you.

Experience has shown that most people who want to be pet sitters do so because they genuinely love animals and like the flexible hours and independent work. It has been said that nursing or teaching takes a special kind of person, and I've found this to be true of pet sitting as well. But, as in any profession, some inspiration is necessary to keep these "naturals" motivated and eager to do a good job for your company. Here are some ways to motivate your pet sitters.

• Institute a sliding scale of compensation. In other words, give your pet sitters some economic incentive. Give small pay increases after every three or six months of reliable service with your company, or whatever your budget can handle and you feel comfortable with.

● Hold sitter contests. Give prizes or cash awards to the pet sitter who sits for the most clients each month, brings in the most new business each quarter, or receives the best evaluation forms from clients each month.

● Give annual Christmas or "appreciation" bonuses to sitters who've done an outstanding job during the year. Sometimes the gesture and recognition means more to employees than the actual amount of the bonus.

● Send out monthly letters to staff members. Tell them of any new business policies or procedures. Inform them of any discounts on services you're now offering. Introduce new staff members. Commend pet sitters who've done an exemplary job. Announce winners of contests. Use the letters to keep sitters informed and motivated. (A sample letter appears after this list.)

● Charge a holiday surcharge for visits (discussed in chapter 3) made on certain nationally recognized holidays. Give the surcharge to the pet sitter as a bonus for working during holiday periods.

● Give pet sitters reduced fees on pet-sitting services from your company.

● Try to arrange a discount for your employees at an area pet supply store or with a local groomer as a company benefit.

● Remember employee birthdays and company anniversaries with a card and/or small gift.

● Use photos of employees in your advertising—they will love the publicity and recognition!

● Recognize pet sitters who have made a suggestion that increased revenues, improved morale or operating procedures, and so on. This can be done in monthly sitter letters, in client newsletters, and during staff meetings.

● Celebrate Professional Pet Sitters' Week (the first full week of March each year) by holding a luncheon for employees or placing an ad in your local newspaper that thanks your hard-working pet sitters.

● Nominate deserving pet sitters for the prestigious Pet Sitter of the Year Award sponsored by Pet Sitters International.

● Invite a hardworking pet sitter to attend PSI's annual convention with you as a reward for their dedication to your company and to the industry.

XYZ Pet Sitters, Inc.
In-Home Pet Sitting Service

Dear XYZ Pet Sitters:

Thank you, thank you, thank you for helping us survive a March that had the flu making the rounds! Many thanks to those who provided substitute sitting services and to those who assisted in taking last-minute reservations for the Easter weekend period. The clients you helped have really expressed their gratefulness and assured me they will be using us again soon!

There are a few things you need to be aware of. Our T-shirt order will arrive April 25. Please make plans to stop by the office to pick up your "summer uniform." These should be great for the upcoming warm weather months!

The luncheon held at The Red Onion Bistro on March 6 in recognition of National Professional Pet Sitters Week was a lot of fun and well-attended. You guys are just the greatest and as I expressed at the luncheon, I really appreciate the terrific job you do as XYZ Pet Sitters!

The Triad Veterinary Emergency Clinic has moved into larger quarters. They are now located at 924 Maple Boulevard, near the I-40 exit ramp. Please make a note of their address—the phone number is the same!

Don't miss this rising star! The daughter of our own Joann Hampton is starring in the Little Theatre's production of "Annie" in the leading role. The play will run April 28–May 14.

Our "Sitter of the Month" is a pet sitter who obviously enjoys her work and is always willing to go the extra mile, according to the client evaluations this office has received! Congratulations Pam Johnson! Keep those eyes and ears open for "running toilets" and coffee pots left on—your customers sure appreciate (and for good reason!) your attentiveness to their homes. Your gift certificate to Oak Valley Mall is enclosed. Enjoy some shopping on XYZ Pet Sitters and know how proud we are to have you on staff!

Bonded
Insured

123 Any Street • Anywhere, U.S.A. 20002
(909) 999-8877 • www.yourwebsite.com

Member of

XYZ Pet Sitters, Inc.

In-Home Pet Sitting Service

Page 2 of 2

Sitters celebrating birthdays this month include Donna Boren (2nd), Bob Williams (8th) and Betsy McGillicutty (24th). Hope each of you will have a very happy day!

It is with much sadness that we must say good-bye this month to a special pet sitter who has worked with us for three and a half years. Debora Leonard, we and your many customers (two-legged and four-legged) are sure going to miss you. But we wish you and your husband, Andy, much luck and happiness with your relocation to the Washington, D.C. area. Please stay in touch!

Because the busy summer months are fast approaching, please let the office know as soon as possible of any dates when you will not be available for sitting assignments. We're receiving many calls already for summer reservations!

Until next month, happy pet sitting!

STAFF MEETINGS

It's important to have regular staff meetings to keep your staff informed, and they can also be good motivators. They enable you to personally interact and communicate, and they give your pet sitters the opportunity to meet each other and compare pet-sitting experiences and knowledge.

I always tried to make my meetings educational as well by inviting a guest speaker to talk about something that would be helpful to my staff members. We had presentations from veterinarians, pet photographers, kennel club spokespeople, humane society personnel, and tax accountants. Our local agricultural extension agent gave an informative talk on the care of houseplants, and our local police demonstrated self-protection techniques. During one staff meeting we watched a dog first-aid video and at another we addressed postcards about our services for a direct mail campaign. Several pet sitters got to know each other well from these meetings and became good friends. The meetings provided a sense of community and the camaraderie was always enjoyable. The refreshments I provided were a way of thanking the sitters for their dedication and good work.

> **Tip**
>
> When a pet sitter leaves, it's wise to notify clients for whom they have worked that they are no longer with your company. It is best to do so in writing. This releases you from any liability if the former sitter continues to pet sit for the customer.

Consider having these meetings as your budget allows. Hold them in your home and make them potluck, if nothing else. It's the sharing of information that will count and benefit your sitters. Plus, it's impressive to clients when they learn that these meetings are held regularly and that education is ongoing for your staff members.

EMPLOYEES OR INDEPENDENT CONTRACTORS?

Your legal relationship with your staff is an extremely important decision you'll need to make. Will the pet sitters who work with you be treated as employees or will you use independent contractors for pet-care services? This is truly one area where you'll be wise to consult with an accountant and an attorney.

The Internal Revenue Service is supposedly taking a hard look at all industries that use independent contractors. Those businesses that are audited and found to have employees instead of independent contractors can incur severe monetary penalties. Learn all you can about what constitutes an employee and what is accepted by the IRS as an independent contractor so you can make an informed decision for your business's personnel needs.

As I have already mentioned, the early trend in the pet-sitting industry was to use independent contractors due to the sometimes seasonal nature of the business and because of the savings in taxes and paperwork. Now, with pet sitting growing in prominence and profits, many business owners are hiring employees so they will have total control of their business and so they don't have to worry about an IRS audit. Thus, this book has been written with more of a slant toward employees. Because I am not an accountant or an attorney, I will not try to advise you in this area, other than to say please do seek good professional counsel on this facet of your business.

Chapter 5

Advertising:
The Means to the Masses

Your office is organized, your staff is trained, your insurance and bond are in effect, and you're ready to begin pet sitting. How do you get that phone ringing with customers requesting your services? You have to get the word out about your business and seize every opportunity you can to educate the public about the valuable in-home pet care you provide.

Advertising is a critical factor in the success of your business. After all, people won't patronize your business if they don't know it exists. I made a mistake in advertising when I opened my pet-sitting business in 1983. I began my business on such a shoestring budget that I had little money left over for advertising. Had I spent more on my initial advertising and reached more people, I'm sure my business would have grown much faster. There is much to be said for the adage that you have to spend money to make money. So, when planning your operating budget, be sure to allot an adequate figure for advertising, especially during your first few years of operation.

Knowing your goals for your business will help you determine your advertising campaign. If you're planning to pet sit to earn some extra spending money, then putting out doorknob hangers on homes in your immediate neighborhood and perhaps running an ad in your neighborhood newspaper will be the only advertising you need to do. However, if your goal is to run a large pet-sitting service that covers the entire city and/or county in which you live, you may want to consider grand opening ads in the local newspaper and spots on a local radio or television station. Advertising costs usually increase with the number of people you want to reach.

As you might expect, the long-standing mass-appeal forms of advertising (television, radio, magazine, newspaper, and billboard) can be overwhelmingly expensive for a small business that is just getting started. However, through my years of experience I've discovered there are many ways to advertise your pet-sitting service that can be very effective and involve only a minimal cost. I'll discuss these inexpensive advertising techniques this chapter, because a penny saved is a penny earned. But first, I want to mention a tremendous advertising tool available to today's pet sitter that I didn't have the benefit of.

PSI'S WEB LOCATOR

There are many good reasons to become a member of PSI. One of the best is that members can choose to be listed on the organization's web site, where pet owners go to look for a pet sitter. All pet owners have to do is type in their zip code and they get a list professional of pet sitters who serve their area. You can see what the search screen looks like below.

While this is strictly a referral service and pet owners are encouraged to interview and do reference checks on any pet sitter they are considering using, it does increase your credibility and visibility to be listed as an organization member. Knowing that you take your career seriously enough to join an educational association is impressive to someone who doesn't know you but is

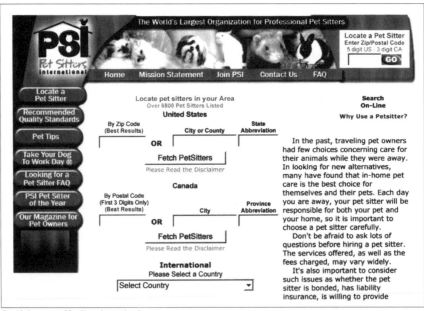

Provided courtesy of Pet Sitters International

exploring the option of using in-home pet care. And obtaining just one client from the PSI Web Locator who repeatedly uses your service can more than pay for your membership dues.

A BROCHURE AND A BUSINESS CARD

Whether you plan to start small or large, I recommend that you have a nicely printed brochure and a business card for your pet-sitting service. Your brochures and business cards will come in handy time and time again in promoting your service. Often, they'll create the first impression of your business so it's important that these materials be well written, attractive, and indicative of your professionalism.

If graphic design is not your area of expertise, hire someone in this field to help you create this literature. There are many freelance designers who may do a good job but charge less than an established advertising or public relations agency. Interview prospective candidates for experience and credentials, look at samples of their work, and shop around for the best deal.

A Great Brochure

A good brochure should contain information about what services your business provides, the advantages it offers for pets and their owners, how it works, and probably, how much it costs. You may also want to include some background material about yourself and/or your pet sitters, including why you started the business, your past experience, and the number of pets in your own household. You'll definitely want your company logo and phone number prominently displayed, and you may want to include a photo of yourself and/or your staff members. Although there will be an initial expense in writing and designing your brochure, it will be money well spent. You'll have a nice brochure representing your business that you can use proudly for years to come.

An added bonus to a well-designed brochure is that you can often take just the front section or a particular portion of it and have it enlarged for use as a flyer or small poster. You'll find an example of how this might work on page 112. Also, most of the copy and graphic design for a brochure can be used on your web site, as well. Just keep in mind while preparing the copy that readers want to know what you can do for them. Be sure this information is told first or is stressed in your written materials, rather than concentrating on your life story.

Something else to keep in mind while preparing your business materials is spelling, punctuation, and grammar. Your materials create an impression not only of your own business, but of our entire industry. We've held brochure contests at national conventions and, as I've perused through entries, I've cringed

RELAX!

ENJOY Your Vacation Knowing Your Pet(s) and Home Are In Our Good Care.

Call:

XYZ Pet Sitters, Inc.

In-Home Pet Sitting Service

- personalized, loving in-home pet care
- make your home look "lived in"
- reasonable rates
- four days notice required
- service available in 27103, 27104, 27106 areas of Winston-Salem

Bonded
Insured

800-111-0000
www.yourwebsite.com

Member of

Tip

A word of caution about using photographs of people: Although they add a personal touch (prospective customers like to see to whom they may be giving a key to their home!), photographs will increase your printing costs and can date a piece of literature. You, or your subjects, should dress generically so the photo will look current with today's styles and fashions. However, when you have a dog under one arm and a cat under another, very little of your clothing will show! Because employees do come and go, it is probably best to picture yourself, as the business owner, on your brochure. Some pet sitters prefer not to place their photo on literature out of concern that it will cause unscrupulous characters to call under the pretense of wanting pet-sitting services.

---

to think that some of this poorly written literature was being distributed to the general public. If your pet-care skills are better than your writing talents, hire a college student majoring in English to compose your text or ask a friend to proof your narrative for typos, misspellings, and double negatives. Your written literature creates a business image that is important to your success—do it right from the start!

Doing it right includes spelling and using the phrase *pet sitting* correctly. According to the dictionary, pet sitting is two words and contains no hyphen when used as a noun or a verb. However, when used as an adjective before a noun, such as "pet-sitting business" or "pet-sitting service," the word is hyphenated.

Business Card Pointers

A simple little business card can be one of the least expensive and most effective tools to promote your service. The first tip is not to leave home without these, since there are myriad ways to use them throughout a day. Other suggestions include:

● Print your business name, phone number, and web address on the card.

● If your office is located in your home, do not print your office address on your business card (or other business materials). Use a P.O. box instead, because you don't want people dropping by your home unexpectedly or with a stray animal.

● Consider adding a company slogan, if you have one, to distinguish yourself from a kennel, groomer, or pet store. Something like *Professional Pet Care When You Can't Be There*.

● If you only work in a certain part of town, list it on the card to cut down on unnecessary calls from areas you don't serve.

● List memberships or affiliations, such as Pet Sitters International, Better Business Bureau, etc.

● Consider using the back of the business card for standards or policies you want to convey, or as a discount coupon. For example, "Use this card for 10 pecent off introductory services of 3 or more pet sitting visits."

A WORD ABOUT "LICENSING"

Of course, you'll want to advertise on your business literature and web site that you are insured and bonded, because these are important selling features of your service. However, *please* don't follow the practice of some pet sitters, who claim that they are "licensed." As of this writing, there is no such thing as licensing for professional pet sitters. Electricians, real estate agents, and hairdressers have to be licensed by their state, but to date this is not true for pet sitters.

The use of the term "licensed" indicates to most people that criteria have been met, usually requiring study and an examination. When a pet sitter uses that word on a brochure, business card, or advertisement, the reference is to the fact that the proper city, county, or home business license or permits have been obtained. Although these types of licenses do indicate that one is running a legally established enterprise, they mean nothing about the skills or education of the pet-sitting professional.

I believe it is misleading to the general public for pet sitters to use "licensed" as if it were a business credential, rather than a form of compliance with city or county taxation laws. I'm not sure how the practice began, but most likely a pet sitter innocently began advertising their business license and then a competitor felt

> **Tip**
>
> In some states, pet sitters who offer pet boarding in a day-care situation must be inspected by the Department of Agriculture and licensed. Using the term "licensed" is meaningful for these pet sitters.

compelled to use the word and the practice snowballed and became common-place in some areas. Because pet sitting involves a lot of old-fashioned honesty, trustworthiness, and ethics, I think pet sitters would be wise not to misrepresent what the term "licensed" means.

A much more meaningful credential for all professional pet sitters is the accreditation program offered by Pet Sitters International. These are home study courses designed and developed by pet sitters and experts in fields of study of practical use to professional pet sitters. It's possible that the government may step in one day with regulations for the pet-sitting industry, so these educational programs are our own attempt at self-regulation. And because the programs do require a course of study and satisfactory completion of an examination, the term "accredited" is much more impressive, and truthful, to the general public.

USING YOUR BROCHURE AND BUSINESS CARDS

Once you have your brochures, flyers, and business cards (all of which list your web site, if you have one), here are some ways they can be used to advertise your services.

Grooming Shops and Pet Supply Stores

Go where the pets are and introduce yourself to the management. Ask for a moment of their time to explain your pet-sitting service, then ask if you may leave your brochures and business cards in a conspicuous location.

Try to develop harmonious relationships with other pet-related businesses. A reciprocal working relationship can be advantageous. Find out if pet supply stores produce a client newsletter in which you might advertise, or ask if the pet supply store is willing to give you and your pet sitters merchandise discounts in exchange

---

Tip

Businesses will be much more receptive to displaying your business cards or brochures if they are presented in a plastic or cardboard stand (available from office supply stores and pet-sitting supply companies). Be sure to tape a business card to the back of the stand. It will identify to whom the stand belongs and will be a permanent display of your name and phone number if all the cards or brochures are taken. Check your displays regularly to make sure they are well filled with literature.

for a free ad in your company newsletter. Discuss the possibility of holding a spring or fall "pet fair" at the pet supply store. (For details, see chapter 6.)

Veterinary Offices and Boarding Kennels

Send a letter of introduction that asks for a personal meeting. (You'll find a sample below.) Then follow up by phone to arrange a mutually convenient appointment time. Don't be afraid to approach veterinarians who offer board-ing facilities for pets or kennel owners. Although you are, in some ways, the competition, hopefully you can establish a harmonious relationship. There will be times when boarding facilities will be completely booked or a vet feels that an older pet should be left at home, and the veterinarian may refer customers to you. Likewise, there may be a time when you are booked or feel a pet needs more medical attention than you are comfortable providing.

A veterinarian who recently spoke at a PSI convention told attendees that if they took their own pets to the vet for regular visits, then most vets would be glad to recommend the pet-sitting service because they knew the pet sitter takes good care of their own pets. She also suggested that pet sitters offer their

---

XYZ Pet Sitters, Inc.
In-Home Pet Sitting Service

Dear Dr. Roberts:

Enclosed please find a brochure about my recently opened pet-sitting business, XYZ Pet Sitters, Inc. We provide in-home pet care in the Winston-Salem/For-syth County area.

Since there may be times when your boarding spaces are filled or instances where you think at-home care is a better option for an elderly pet, I hope that we can work together. Reciprocally I may be able to refer new business to you as often we pet sit for newcomers to the community who have yet to establish a relationship with a veterinarian.

I would appreciate a few minutes of your time to get acquainted and learn more about your hospital. I will call you next week to schedule a convenient time and look forward to talking with you further.

Very truly yours,
XYZ Pet Sitters, Inc.

Member of

Bonded   123 Any Street • Anywhere, U.S.A. 20002
Insured   (909) 999-8877 • www.yourwebsite.com

pet-sitting services for free to veterinarians to show appreciation for referrals and to let the vet experience firsthand the good pet care delivered.

Extending the hand of friendship should be an easy task for today's new pet sitter. The industry has become sufficiently established so that the boarding industry realizes pet sitters are here to stay and that there are advantages to working together. I've even had several kennel owners attend my pet-sitting seminars and the annual PSI convention, who told me they realized at-home pet care was the trend of the future and they were adding it to their existing operation to be a more full-service business. I, and other pet sitters, have also had veterinarians tell us they were glad we were providing at-home pet-care services. They explained they actually believed it was better for pets to remain in a familiar, comfortable environment and only had boarding facilities because previously there had not been an alternative for pet owners. They said they much preferred to keep their limited boarding spaces available for pets who require medical care. Although every vet or kennel owner may not greet you with open arms, I think you'll find the majority will be receptive to your friendly overtures.

A word of advice, though: If you sincerely want to build good relationships with boarding industry members, do not engage in negative advertising. Don't depict a dog behind bars on your brochure, as if that is what going to a boarding kennel is like, and don't use the phrase "kennel cough" as stereotypical of a kennel. It's hard to win friends when you're referring to them negatively. Several kennel owners have shared with me that they are offended and insulted when pet sitters use such tactics.

It is much more professional to advertise the positive features of at-home pet care and enjoy a good rapport with other pet-care professionals. After all, some pets do well and enjoy being boarded; others are happier in the home environment. With more than 60 percent of American households owning some type of pet, there is enough business out there for everyone! Establishing a cooperative relationship with local veterinarians and boarding kennels can be very beneficial for all concerned, including the pets and their owners. It also speaks well for your professionalism.

Travel Agencies

Visit or write to all the travel agencies in your community, informing them of your services. You'll find sample letters of introduction on pages 118 and 119. Travel agents often do a lot of traveling—plus, they can certainly connect you with the traveling public! Supply them with your brochures and business cards. A trifold brochure fits neatly into the jacket of an airline ticket.

XYZ Pet Sitters, Inc.

In-Home Pet Sitting Service

Dear Employees of Vacation Travel Agency:

Enclosed is information describing our personalized home pet-care service, XYZ Pet Sitters, Inc. We would appreciate it if you would circulate or post our brochure in your office. Our service may make traveling much easier for many of your clients!

We are happy to provide you with additional brochures upon request. We look forward to serving you and your customers and appreciate any referrals.

Sincerely yours,
XYZ Pet Sitters

Member of

Bonded
Insured

123 Any Street • Anywhere, U.S.A. 20002
(909) 999-8877 • www.yourwebsite.com

Consider offering each travel agent an incentive (coupons redeemable for your services or even $5 per customer who uses your services). A sample is on page 120. Another idea is to offer clients of the travel agent a special introductory fee on the use of your services.

Humane Societies, Dog Clubs, Cat Associations, and Rescue Groups

Write to these organizations, enclosing your brochures and business cards. Offer one free pet-sitting visit to anyone who adopts a pet through your local Humane Society, or offer dog club members an introductory discount on their first use of your services. These are important groups to notify about your business; the chances are great that individuals associated with them are true animal lovers who most likely will need your service at some time. You'll find a sample notification letter on page 81 of chapter 4.

XYZ Pet Sitters, Inc.

In-Home Pet Sitting Service

During the months of April, May, and June, XYZ Pet Sitters, Inc., is having a special promotional campaign for travel agents. Since 1983, we have been providing the best in personalized home pet care to residents faced with traveling. In an effort to increase our business, we are offering the following promotion to local travel agents because you know best who may be in need of our services.

- A $5 commission to each new customer you refer to us who books our services for a minimum of three visits. This $5 referral fee will be paid the first of each month (May, June and July) directly to the agent responsible for sending the client to us.

- A 10 percent introductory discount will be extended to your clients who use our services as a result of your referral (new clients only).

Brochures describing our services and discount coupons (which the referring agent will sign) will be provided by XYZ Pet Sitters, Inc., for your use during this campaign. The brochures will easily fit inside the jackets of airline tickets, business envelopes and so on. Your participation could include asking your clients if they have pets that will need to be cared for, or simply inserting literature about our services in your mailers. You determine how actively you participate in our promotional campaign.

I hope you will take part in the promotion—we can all benefit from it. Your agents can earn extra money, your clients will appreciate the discount extended through your agency, and our list of satisfied customers will grow. Please call us at 999-8877 by April 3, 20__ if you want to participate in this campaign and we'll get brochures and coupons to you promptly. I look forward to working with you this spring!

Very truly yours,
Patti J. Moran
President

Member of

Bonded
Insured

123 Any Street • Anywhere, U.S.A. 20002
(909) 999-8877 • www.yourwebsite.com

XYZ Pet Sitters, Inc.

XYZ Pet Sitters, Inc., is pleased to extend a 10 percent introductory discount to the clients of _____.

This coupon must be presented when a house key is picked up by XYZ Pet Sitters, Inc., and is valid only for services consisting of three of more visits per home.

Expires 12/31/___
Travel Agent

Newcomers to Your Area

These are people you always want to reach because they probably don't know their neighbors well enough to ask them to look after their pets. "Home" is probably somewhere else, so many newcomers will most likely travel for holidays. How do you reach them?

Call your local chamber of commerce and inform them about your business (or consider joining the chamber of commerce if the benefits of membership are worth the annual membership dues). Often, chambers of commerce or visitors' centers will have lists of new people moving to the area that they may share with you. Or contact your local welcome wagon, newcomers' club, or similar groups with information on your services.

Real estate agencies sell homes to newcomers all the time, so mail your brochure to all the realtors in your community, along with a letter such as the one on page 121. Also, a growing service in many communities makes moving easy by seeing that utilities are hooked up and turned on for newcomers. If such a service exists in your area, ask the service operators if they would tell newcomers with pets about your business. I know of one pet sitter who learns about newcomers by checking the water connections, which are city public records.

Regardless of how you find newcomers, don't miss out on the business they can provide. And once you've figured out who they are, try sending them a welcoming letter such as the one on page 122 that, of course, introduces your service.

XYZ Pet Sitters, Inc.

In-Home Pet Sitting Service

Dear Employees of ABC Realtors:

Enclosed is our brochure describing our services to the community. I think we may be of service to you while you are taking vacations, business trips or working overtime. Your pet-owning clients may also find our services of special interest. We would appreciate it if you could circulate or post our brochure in your company.

Please keep our service in mind as you sell real estate to newcomers in our area who are pet owners. We would be happy to furnish you with additional brochures upon request.

Thank you for your time and consideration.

Sincerely,
XYZ Pet Sitters, Inc.

Member of

Bonded
Insured

123 Any Street • Anywhere, U.S.A. 20002
(909) 999-8877 • www.yourwebsite.com

Housecleaning and Lawn-Care Services

Using the Yellow Pages, write to all these types of services with information about your pet-sitting business. The people who do this type of work visit homes every day. They know who has pets and can spread word of your services or leave a brochure for their clients. You could also ask if they would include your brochure with their next billing, or if they would rent their mailing list to you. Some may remember what it was like when they started out and sympathetically give your service a plug, but you should offer something (money, discounts, reciprocal referrals) in return for this help.

Garden Clubs

Obtain a list of the garden clubs in your service area and write to them, enclosing your brochure. Even if club members don't have pets, they probably have plants that need water and care when they're away from home. Remember that

XYZ Pet Sitters, Inc.

In-Home Pet Sitting Service

Dear Newcomer:

Welcome to your new home! We hope you will enjoy our city and all it has to offer. As lifelong residents of the area, we can truly say this is a great place to live and work. We hope you'll soon agree!

In the event that you are a pet owner or a potential pet owner, we want to make you aware of XYZ Pet Sitters, Inc. We find that new residents face a problem with what to do with their pets when traveling on business or pleasure. Often, there is no family close by to call on, and neighbors take a while to get to know. In any event, we want to make you aware of our service and hope you'll take the time to read the enclosed brochure, which explains our business in more detail. You can rest assured that each staff member is bonded and insured.

Again, welcome to the area. Please call us if we may be of service to you.

Sincerely,
XYZ Pet Sitters, Inc.

Member of

Bonded
Insured

123 Any Street • Anywhere, U.S.A. 20002
(909) 999-8877 • www.yourwebsite.com

---

anyone who hears about your service may tell someone else, creating a grapevine effect. This is how you can inexpensively get the word out that you're in business. You'll find a sample of this type of letter on page 123.

Law Enforcement Agencies

It is a smart business practice to inform your local police and sheriff's department of the valuable crime-deterrent measures your service provides. If your community has a Crime Stop or Neighborhood Watch program, law enforcement personnel may spread the word about your services. And, heaven forbid, if you arrive to find a client's home has been burglarized and call law enforcement officials, they will be familiar with your business. Page 124 has a sample of the letter I used to inform law enforcement officials about my new business.

XYZ Pet Sitters, Inc.

In-Home Pet Sitting Service

Dear Maple Leaf Garden Club:

Enclosed you will find brochures describing services provided by XYZ Pet Sitters, Inc. Although our primary function is personalized home pet care while the owner is away, we also are happy to provide loving care for your plants. Prices are based on travel and time involved; however, we are reasonable!

We are a locally owned and operated business, and we are bonded and insured. We would appreciate so much your announcing our service at your next club meeting. We hope we may be of service to your members in the near future.

Sincerely yours,
XYZ Pet Sitters

Member of

Bonded   123 Any Street • Anywhere, U.S.A. 20002
Insured   (909) 999-8877 • www.yourwebsite.com

Friends and Family Members

Get your brochures to everyone who knows you and will support you in your new venture. Everybody knows or works with someone who has a pet, and that someone just may be interested in using your services. A personal recommendation also means a lot in this business, so get your friends and family members to spread the word about your unique service.

Local Businesses and Companies

Obtain a list from your local chamber of commerce of the major employers in your area. Then send your brochure to the personnel departments of these companies. Often benefits managers in these departments are on the lookout for services and information that will be useful to their employees. They may

XYZ Pet Sitters, Inc.

In-Home Pet Sitting Service

Dear Chief _____ :

Enclosed you will find information describing XYZ Pet Sitters, Inc. Our service involves going into customers' homes to care for their pets while they are away on vacation or business. We feel that an important part of our service is giving the home a lived-in look by bringing in mail and newspapers, opening and closing curtains and alternating lights—all measures that we hope will be crime deterrents. Although we certainly hope we never encounter a home that has been burglarized, in the event that we do, our staff has been instructed to leave the premises immediately and contact appropriate law enforcement officials.

As spring and summer approach, we anticipate being very busy in the city and county area. For this reason we wanted to make you and your department aware of our service and our sincere desire to have a good working relationship with the police department. If our brochures can be incorporated into any of the community-watch or crime-stoppers programs, we will be happy to supply literature or assist in any way we can. Each of our pet sitters is bonded, insured, reliable, responsible and hard working.

We appreciate the fine efforts of your department and thank you for notifying your staff that our service is available.

Should you or your departmental members have any further questions regarding XYZ Pet Sitters, Inc., please give us a call.

Sincerely yours,
XYZ Pet Sitters, Inc.

Member of

Bonded
Insured

123 Any Street • Anywhere, U.S.A. 20002
(909) 999-8877 • www.yourwebsite.com

XYZ Pet Sitters, Inc.

In-Home Pet Sitting Service

Dear Employees of Atlas Law Offices:

Enclosed is our brochure describing how we can be of service to you while you are taking vacations, business trips or working over-time.

We would appreciate it if you would circulate or post our brochure on an employee bulletin board or mention us in your company newsletter. Please call if you need more information or additional brochures.

Thank you for your time and consideration.

Sincerely yours,
XYZ Pet Sitters, Inc.

Member of

Bonded
Insured

123 Any Street • Anywhere, U.S.A. 20002
(909) 999-8877 • www.yourwebsite.com

print a blurb about your service in their company newsletter or post your brochure on employee bulletin boards or in the company cafeteria. Consider offering an introductory discount to their employees for a limited time, to make their communication efforts worthwhile. Above, you'll find a copy of the letter I sent to corporations.

Civic Clubs and Nonprofit Organizations

Obtain a list of these from your local chamber of commerce and, again, send your brochure and an introductory letter to each. On page 126 you'll find a sample of an introductory letter. By offering their members an introductory discount, you may entice them to announce your business and circulate your brochure at their next group meeting.

If you're comfortable with public speaking, offer to give a talk about your new business at their club's next scheduled meeting. Guest speakers are often in demand, and you'll find most audiences will be interested in your talk and

XYZ Pet Sitters, Inc.

In-Home Pet Sitting Service

Dear Arts Council Members:

Enclosed you will find our brochure, which describes the services of XYZ Pet Sitters, Inc. We have been caring for pets in the area since 1983. We are trying to reach all pet owners in the community before the summer vacation season begins. We would appreciate so much your circulation of our brochure at your next meeting. Any member of your organization using our service before _____ will receive a 10 percent discount on our services. (He or she must identify him or herself as a member of your organization.)

Please call if you need more brochures or if we can provide additional information.

Sincerely yours,
XYZ Pet Sitters, Inc.

Member of

Bonded
Insured

123 Any Street • Anywhere, U.S.A. 20002
(909) 999-8877 • www.yourwebsite.com

appreciative of your visit. Plus, after meeting you personally, some group members will feel confident about giving your service a try. If just the thought of public speaking gets your knees shaking, remember that most people share this fear to some degree. The fact that you're willing to get up and talk about your business will be admired, and after a few speeches, you'll be a lot more at ease with making public presentations.

Apartment Complexes

Using the Yellow Pages, call all apartment complexes in your service area to determine which ones allow pets. Then send your brochure to the apartment managers of these complexes and ask that they inform resident pet owners of your services. Many apartment complexes provide a welcome packet of information to new residents, and your brochure can be added. Ask about this possibility. A copy of the letter I mailed to apartment complex managers is on page 127.

XYZ Pet Sitters, Inc.
In-Home.Pet Sitting Service

Dear Manager of Cross Creek Apartments:

Enclosed is our brochure describing the services of XYZ Pet Sitters, Inc. We have been caring for pets in the area since 1983. Because your apartment complex allows pets, we would appreciate your posting our brochure in a conspicuous location. Please let me know if you would be interested in incorporating our brochure into your apartment's welcome material for new residents. I will be happy to provide you with additional brochures.

Thank you for spreading the word about our services. We look forward to caring for the pets at your apartment complex.

Sincerely yours,
XYZ Pet Sitters, Inc.

Member of

Bonded
Insured

123 Any Street • Anywhere, U.S.A. 20002
(909) 999-8877 • www.yourwebsite.com

Condominium Complexes

Condominiums, town homes, cluster homes, and gated communities are springing up everywhere. My experience has shown that these homes appeal to young professionals who may travel a lot for work and may be in need of your services, and to the older population who are empty nesters (except for the pets!) and want to downsize. Most of these residential complexes have a homeowner's association as their governing board, which is made up of residents. Get your brochures to these board members for display in their clubhouse or inclusion in their resident newsletter.

> ### Tip
>
> Do not go out and stuff brochures into mailboxes or doorways. Stuffing mailboxes (without postage and mail service) is a crime, and most apartments and condominiums adhere to a strict no-solicitation policy. You can create a negative image of your business by engaging in these tactics.

Bulletin Boards

You may not have noticed these before, but they are available in many places. Grocery stores, restaurants, laundromats, and recreation facilities often have one available for the public's use. Start looking for (and encourage your sitters to do the same) and taking advantage of these to post your business card, brochure, flyer, or just a notice such as the one below. It's a great form of free advertising!

Local Colleges and Schools

These institutions have employees and students (and bulletin boards) who are likely to be pet owners. Send your brochure to the language, anthropology, archeology, and geography departments (to name a few) at these schools. Professors often organize field trips, and someone in their group may be glad to know your service is only a phone call or e-mail away!

As these ideas illustrate, there are numerous ways to make the public aware of your pet-sitting service. So, now that I've convinced you of the advertising value found in a brochure, business card, business letterhead, and postage stamp, let's move on to other advertising techniques.

XYZ Pet Sitters, Inc.

In-Home Pet Sitting Service

123 Any Street • Anywhere, U.S.A. 20002
(909) 999-8877

You Can Trust Your Pet to Us

- Feed, Water and Exercise Your Pets
- In The Comfort of Your Home
- Individual Loving Attention
- Make Your Home Look "Lived In"

Bonded
Insured

Member of

INEXPENSIVE WAYS TO ADVERTISE

Very early on, I learned that pet owners come in all shapes and sizes, from different economic levels, and with a wide range of interests. So it's difficult—and unwise—to pinpoint one specific group for advertising purposes. The one thing pet owners do have in common is a genuine love of their pets. Keep this in mind and try to reach all types of pet owners in your advertising efforts.

● **Plastic badges.** Invest a few dollars in a plastic lapel badge that has your business name, logo, and your name printed on it. Wear it all the time! People read these, and you'll be amazed at the number of times people will inquire about your occupation. Store clerks, wait staff, and post office personnel are just a few who asked about my pet-sitting service simply from reading my badge.

● **Magnetic car signs.** These are a bit more expensive than plastic lapel badges, but well worth their cost in the advertising they generate for your business. My car signs received so much attention and brought in so many new customers, I wish I had invested in them when first opening my business. I highly recommend you give this purchase top priority in your advertising budget. If you drive a truck or all-terrain vehicle, consider having a magnetic strip made for the back. Drivers behind you at stoplights will then be jotting your phone number down. Shop around for the best price on magnetic signs. Of course, when you're driving around town with your business signs for all the world to see, make sure you drive in a careful manner. As noted earlier, you don't want people associating XYZ Pet Sitters with speed demons.

> **Tip**
>
> Wear your badge when going to a customer's home for an initial interview. It lets the customer know who's at the door and presents an official and professional image for a sitter.

> **Tip**
>
> When making pet-sitting rounds, take the magnetic signs off your car. Otherwise, your clients and their homes will not remain confidential, as you have assured them they will be. The signs are easy to remove and replace on your car doors.

● **Personalized license plates.** These have become very popular in recent years and, just like the magnetic car signs, they provide a terrific form of relatively inexpensive advertising. Although some pet sitters do not like vanity license plates because they're afraid the plate advertises that the homes they're parked outside are unoccupied, I thought the exposure they provided to drivers behind me at stoplights was more beneficial than the likelihood of causing a burglary at someone's home. And I was often approached for a business card by someone who read my license plate in the parking lot of a supermarket or shopping center. You'll have to determine if this is a good advertising idea in your area.

● **Costumes.** Rent (or make) a cute animal costume and then walk the city streets during lunch hours, handing out your brochures. A cute costumed "animal" (you or someone you've hired) may show up at all kinds of places. Of course, you'll need to get permission for a costumed pet to appear, but investigate the possibilities of outdoor concerts, children's story hours at the library (parents go, too), craft fairs, street festivals, and dog and cat shows. It's a relatively inexpensive and well-received means of advertising.

● **T-shirts or sweatshirts.** With the popularity of T-shirts and sweatshirts these days, a well-designed shirt will advertise your business for you. I had numerous people stop me to inquire about our services after reading my shirt. Plus, they make a great pet-sitting "uniform" that can easily be laundered. Your customers may be interested in your shirts, too, so company T-shirts could be profitable. Shop around before placing an order; prices vary.

● **City or county tax office.** Most counties require dog owners to list dogs and pay the appropriate tax assessed on these pets. Dog tags are issued to pet owners from this annual tax listing. You may be able to purchase (or copy) names and addresses of dog owners from your tax office's master list. You could then mail these pet owners information about your pet-sitting service. Time and money will be required to do a mass mailing of this sort, but it's a great way of directly reaching people who may need your services. Taking this idea a step further, you can include a pre-sitting questionnaire with your mailing. This could be a postcard-size form that dog owners could quickly fill out and mail back, indicating preliminary interest in your services. The business this mailing may generate could far exceed the costs involved. Discuss with your local post office the option of making these forms "postage paid by addressee" to make it easier for potential customers to use and return the surveys to you. Or, consider hiring a mailing house to handle this bulk-mailing program for you. They can also advise you about postage options and costs.

● **Programs and bulletins.** Explore the many activities in your community that use printed programs with advertising space. Some of these include local theater programs, high school sports programs, symphony sponsors, professional/minor league sports promotions, Junior League newsletters, ski or diving club bulletins, and a host of others. Advertising on this smaller scale is generally cheaper than other media and gives you a known target group. You can also use these advertisements to offer introductory discounts to ski club members, for example, or to symphony season ticket holders.

● **Posters.** Posters can also be helpful in getting the word out about your business. Because they are generally larger than a business flyer or brochure, they are more easily noticed on community bulletin boards. You may want to check into the cost of having some of these printed for your business. Include tear-off phone number strips along the bottom of your promotional posters, as shown in the example on page 132. This gives you a way to see if the advertising is working for you, and it's convenient for viewers who are interested in your services but may not have a pen available to take down your phone number. I know of some pet sitters who have their posters printed in a pad form. This enables interested pet owners to simply tear off a flyer.

● **Specialty items.** These items include magnets, pens, pet food can lids, key chains, and pet-theme calendars, to name a few that can be imprinted with the name of your business. Although such items are a good form of advertising, they become expensive when given out to the general public. My experience has shown that most pet sitters use the specialty items as a way to say thank you to their clients. They mail a calendar with an annual holiday card, or they leave a refrigerator magnet during the last visit of a sitting assignment. Such items also make nice giveaways at pet fairs or business expositions. If you look into specialty items for your business, it's a good idea to shop around for the best price.

● **Gift certificates.** You're sure to be approached for donations to area fund-raisers by civic groups, churches, and other groups. Consider donating a gift certificate for a weekend of free pet sitting or for a dollar amount that can be redeemed by the recipient. You usually receive free advertising in exchange for the donation, and I found the contribution usually resulted in the recipient becoming a repeat customer. This repeat business more than paid for the donated services—plus, the donation was a legitimate business expense. However, give some thought to your policy on such contributions. There are a lot of fund-raising organizations that will be asking for your support.

RELAX!

ENJOY Your Vacation Knowing Your Pet(s) and Home Are In Our Good Care.

Call:

XYZ Pet Sitters, Inc.

In-Home Pet Sitting Service

- personalized, loving in-home pet care
- make your home look "lived in"
- reasonable rates
- four days notice required
- service available in 27103, 27104, 27106 areas of Winston-Salem

Bonded
Insured

Member of

(909) 999-8877   (909) 999-8877   (909) 999-8877   (909) 999-8877   (909) 999-8877   (909) 999-8877   (909) 999-8877   (909) 999-8877   (909) 999-8877   (909) 999-8877   (909) 999-8877   (909) 999-8877   (909) 999-8877   (909) 999-8877   (909) 999-8877   (909) 999-8877   (909) 999-8877   (909) 999-8877

• **Adopt-a-Highway.** Many states have implemented this kind of program to help keep roads and highways "clean and green." Area businesses adopt a certain section of a road or highway and agree to regularly clean litter from the sides of it. In exchange, the state will erect a road sign that states the name of the business responsible for that portion of road or highway. This is valuable advertising as well as a good program to become involved in. Contact your state department of transportation to see if this program exists.

• **"Lead groups."** These groups, also known as networks, are a new marketing phenomenon in many cities. A "lead group" consists of a variety of business people or entrepreneurs who meet weekly or monthly for a breakfast, lunch, or social hour. The purpose of the group is to help build each other's businesses by sharing business leads. Usually a lead club allows only one member from an occupation to belong, for example, one insurance agent, exterminator, printing company, plumber, banker, and so on. The club members use the businesses and services of their lead group members when applicable, and refer friends, family, and coworkers. It's a great way to meet area professionals and advertise your pet-sitting services. The membership costs are usually nominal and most cities have several such clubs from which to choose. If a pet-sitting firm already belongs to the first club you contact, try another one—or start a new lead group! Check the business section of your newspaper or Yellow Pages for these networking groups.

DO YOU NEED A WEB SITE?

Traditionally, the best way to reach a large number of people with your advertising message has been through newspaper, radio, television, and Yellow Pages ads. However, these are usually the most expensive forms of advertising and, unless your goal is to operate a larger-scale pet-sitting service, there's really no reason to reach the masses. To do so would only waste your revenues and time as you answer phone calls only to tell callers that you don't serve their neighborhood or that you're not taking new clients now.

If your plan is to pet sit on a small scale, the less expensive advertising ideas should work well for you. Some of these ideas, along with word of mouth, will soon build your clientele to the point you want. But whether you're a small, midsize, or large pet-sitting service, you'll probably want a web site for your business. So before I share my experience with and opinions on the four traditional, expensive advertising media, let's touch again on web sites and how most pet sitters structure them.

Building Your Web Site

Establishing a web site helps the smaller pet-sitting operation look more business savvy, and helps the larger operation reach a wider audience with a longer-lasting message that can be less expensive than the traditional advertising methods. Costs involved will depend upon whether you do it yourself or hire a web site designer, and also on how extensive, complex, and sophisticated your web pages are. Web designers charge either by the project, by the hour, or by the page.

Study existing web sites to get an idea of layouts and formats you like, so you'll have an idea of what you're looking for before meeting with web designers. Work out the content for your site, as well. This way they can more accurately estimate costs for you.

While some pet sitters tell me they were able to figure out web site design pretty easily from purchased software packages, I believe in letting people do what they do best. Thus, if you're as computer illiterate as I am but want a nice-looking web site, call a web site designer.

Here are some ideas of the kinds of information you will want on your web site. Besides a home page and a "contact us" feature, these are the basic topics included on most pet sitter web sites.

Advantages of Using Your Service

- For the pet

- For the pet's owner

Services Provided

- Pet sitting and what's included

- Overnights and what's included

- Midday dog walks: length of walk, number of dogs walked simultaneously, etc.

Rates

- Specials or packages available

Company Policies

- Hours of pet-sitting visits

- Cancellation fees

- Holiday surcharges

- Last-minute-reservation surcharges

- Returned check fees

About Us

- The owner

- Staff member info or requirements

- Memberships and affiliations

Our Customers

- Pictures of clients' pets

- Testimonials from pleased customers (with permission!)

More elaborate sites offer links to other pet-related sites, travel tips, a "lost and found pets" section, and a list of any specialized services provided, such as e-mail updates while the client is away. As of this writing, a few services have business forms online that enable clients to make reservations or pay invoices. These are more the exception than the rule, though.

An advantage of a web site as an advertising method is that once you have it prepared and hosted online, your message is out there. It's more of an up-front investment that will continue to work for you, unlike a newspaper ad that is quickly discarded. Yes, there will be some maintenance to keep a web site current, but it's a cost of doing business in today's world.

NEWSPAPERS

Advertising in the newspaper will get you results. But before you take out an expensive display ad, try this suggestion first. Send out a news release (there's a sample on page 136). Using news releases is such a good idea that it's worth repeating. Deliver or mail your news release to the business editor of your local newspaper(s). The openings of new businesses are often considered newsworthy enough to rate a free paragraph on the business page. Some smaller or rural newspapers will even run a full-fledged article free, announcing the opening and details of your business.

If pet sitting is a relatively new concept in your area, your business may intrigue newspaper reporters. From a human interest standpoint, pet sitting has the potential to make a good story. Your service can be approached from the

XYZ Pet Sitters, Inc.
In-Home Pet Sitting Service

Date: For further information contact:
For: XYZ Pet Sitters, Inc.   Jane Smith, President
For Release: Immediately

New Pet-Sitting Business Opens in Piedmont

Winston-Salem, N. C. . . . Area pet owners now have an alternate choice for pet care during vacation and business trips. Jane Smith, president, has opened XYZ Pet Sitters, Inc., at 1234 Anywhere Street. The unique service provided by the company means that pet owners can now leave their household pet(s) in the comfort and familiarity of home.

"One of our insured and bonded staff members will visit a home on a daily basis to feed, water and care for the pet(s). And, most importantly, we'll provide lots of tender loving care and personalized attention during each visit," says Smith, president of the newly formed company.

XYZ Pet Sitters, Inc., has a staff of eight professional pet sitters, all of whom truly love pets and have been thoroughly trained by the company. Not only do they all look after household pets in pampered style, they also are happy to bring in newspapers, mail and even water houseplants. "We want every pet owner to be able to leave home with peace of mind, knowing his or her pet(s) and home are in our responsible care," notes Smith.

All clients making reservations for pet-sitting services during the month of May will receive a 10-percent discount off the total sitting fee. "This offer is to introduce our services to Piedmont pet owners and is part of our grand opening celebration," says Smith. To get additional information or to make a reservation, call XYZ Pet Sitters, Inc., at 999-8811.

Member of

Bonded   123 Any Street • Anywhere, U.S.A. 20002
Insured   (909) 999-8877 • www.yourwebsite.com

Tip

If you operate your pet-sitting service in an extremely large city, newspaper advertising may not be the wisest use of your advertising dollar. First, the cost may be prohibitive. Second, it may result in an annoying number of crank calls. Third, you may not even cover the entire city with your pet-sitting services. So give careful thought before using any form of mass media advertising. And when you do, be sure to specify the areas you serve to make maximum use of your advertising dollar.

---

angle of its uniqueness, its potential to deter crime, or its female ownership (if applicable). Call reporters assigned to human interest articles (including those at radio and television stations) to inquire if anyone would like to interview you for a story. If so, you're on your way. Often these stories do more to promote your business and lend credibility than any amount of paid advertising. (For more information on news releases, please see "News Releases" in chapter 6.)

Even if you get free media coverage, you may still need to buy some advertising. An inexpensive form of newspaper advertising is to run a short classified ad about your service under the "Pets" heading. Page 138 shows some sample classified ads.

These classified ads are great because they say a lot in only a few words. However, before running similar copy, make sure you can count on a good reference from area veterinarians and that you are bonded and insured. And if you decide to use wording similar to the sample ads on page 138, be sure you are also running an ad in the Yellow Pages. The idea behind doing both is that most people turn to the Yellow Pages when they are looking for a service provider, so it can add extra weight to your little newspaper classified ad to point out you also have a Yellow Pages ad running. In addition, whether deserved or not, some people think a Yellow Pages ad lends credibility to a business. The classified ad sounds meatier and gets you additional bang for your Yellow Pages ad dollar. If you have a web site, you may want to say (in addition, or instead), "Please visit us at www.WeLovePets.com!"

Some newspapers have a "Consumer Review" or "Business Review" section that, for a fee, will run an article and picture about your business. These are sometimes called advertorials. Check to see if your newspaper publishes neighborhood inserts or a special pet page section. If so, ads in these sections are usually less expensive because the inserts only reach readers in certain zip codes. I

Looking for a pet sitter?
Ask your vet about us.
XYZ Pet Sitters, Inc. 999-8877.
Bonded and insured.

Need a pet sitter? See our
display ad on page 345 of
the Yellow Pages. XYZ Pet
Sitters, Inc. 999-8877.

advertised in each of these sections many times and always received an excellent response.

The most successful newspaper advertising campaign I ran for my business became what is now called "PZZZ . . . Ads." These were a series of ads depicting photos of a pet in holiday or seasonal attire with a short phrase imparting a message about my services. The photos were eye-catching and humorous, and increased my business tremendously. The ad series was very popular with pet owners, and even with people who had no pets. One woman told me she didn't have any pets but she loved my cute ads so much that she clipped them each week and posted them on her office bulletin board for coworkers to see. These "PZZZ . . . Ads" are now available for purchase (see the appendix for ordering information). If you prefer to design your own display ads, a small one with a catchy phrase underneath, such as "Holiday Travel?" or "Business Travel?" or "Going on Vacation?" will also get noticed.

When the American Animal Hospital Association (AAHA) asked who cares for the family cat or dog, their findings showed that in 66 percent of American families, it's Mom. I found this to be true in the ten years I operated my pet-sitting business—seven out of ten calls for services were usually made by the woman in the household. Keep this in mind when targeting your newspaper advertising. If your newspaper has a daily or weekly women's, home, or food section, these could be good places for your ad. Advertising in the travel, entertainment, sports, and business sections can also be effective.

I found advertising in Sunday through Wednesday papers to bring a better response than Thursday through Saturday, because those are the days people tend to travel and, therefore, miss the daily local newspaper. Because display advertising tends to be expensive, I primarily advertised before holidays, during the summer vacation months, and on the anniversary date of my business opening. (Announcing the birthday or age of your business lends further credibility—it shows you have staying power and are not a fly-by-night operation.)

Newspaper advertising does get noticed and creates name recognition with repetition. If the ad is distinctive, people will remember it long after the newspaper has been discarded.

When possible, plan your newspaper advertising months in advance to take advantage of contract rates, which is discounted pricing in exchange for a commitment to advertise a certain number of times over several weeks—for example, running four ads in an eight-week period. If you know you'll be advertising all summer, ask your advertising sales representative about contract rates.

YELLOW PAGES

Advertising in the Yellow Pages of your local telephone directory is another way of reaching a mass audience. Although it is expensive for a small business, it's a necessary expenditure, especially when you're just getting started. This is because people who need a service often consult the Yellow Pages for providers.

In the past, pet sitters had little choice about the placement of Yellow Pages ads. We were automatically lumped under the heading of "Kennels" or "Dog and Cat Boarding/Exercising," although neither accurately reflects the care we provide. This has not been all bad, though. After all, with pet sitting still a new concept, many pet owners aren't aware of our personalized services and don't know to look for us, unless they see our listing with the more traditional boarding or kennel option. With pet sitting growing and gaining in popularity, more telephone books offer the option of listing under "Pet Sitters" or "Sitting Services." It's a good idea to have a dual listing under "Pet Sitters" and "Kennels," if both are available to you.

In the first year or two of your business, you need an enticing display ad, or at least something larger than the normal, free phone listing a business receives. You want to let the world know your service is available. After you've established a reputation, just your business name, number, and perhaps a descriptive slogan in the Yellow Pages will suffice.

My initial experience with advertising in the Yellow Pages was not especially positive (perhaps clouded by an overly aggressive salesperson). But the results of advertising surveys—of my own pet-sitting clients and of other pet-sitting firms—have shown that Yellow Pages ads are consistently among the top five methods of bringing in new customers. Usually it's a year-long advertising contract with the Yellow Pages that can seem like a tremendous expense to the small business owner, but just consider it a necessary part of being in a service business.

RADIO

I had mixed feelings about this form of advertising. Calls for our services did come in on the days my radio commercials were broadcast. However, I'm not convinced that the amount of business generated from these commercials paid for the high cost of airing them. Radio advertising is expensive for a small business owner; I recommend that you wait until after you've gotten your business off the ground and have some advertising dollars to spare.

If you decide to pursue radio advertising, keep some things in mind. First, do your homework by calling and researching various radio stations. Request Arbitron ratings from each station. Arbitron is a company that conducts private surveys to determine which groups of people listen to what radio station and when they listen. Arbitron periodically publishes these demographic statistics about the listeners for each station. By obtaining this information, you can most effectively determine the right station and time to place your commercial.

When selecting radio stations, choose the ones whose audience profile matches your potential customer. Choosing the station you listen to or the one that happens to be the least expensive is not necessarily your best buy. Also, there's no sense in paying a premium price to advertise on a station that covers four counties if you don't provide service to those areas, even if the station is the most popular.

I found that running radio commercials during rush-hour traffic is the most effective time. You reach the working person who takes vacations, may travel on business, and presumably can afford your service.

Monday, Tuesday, and Wednesday were the best days to run my radio commercials. As with newspaper ads, the logic is that Thursday through Sunday are more popular vacation days, and your listening audience may not be as large. You want to reach the vacationers before they leave town.

Because talk radio has become so popular in recent years, a better option would be to find out which local radio talk shows broadcast in your area. Then send news releases, along with a cover letter offering to be a guest on any business, pet, or community service programs. If you're invited to appear on a talk program, the exposure and credibility it lends would be far more valuable than any commercial you could pay to run. And such appearances will help establish you as an expert in your field. The media will soon begin calling you when they need a spokesperson on pets or pet sitting—more free advertising!

TELEVISION

Some time ago I attended a workshop for small businesses. A local advertising executive spoke. After his presentation, I told him about my pet-sitting service and asked where I should put my advertising dollars. His emphatic reply was television. I gasped, thinking big money, but he pointed out that families have pets and families stay at home and watch television. Families also take vacations. He pointed out that retired people and homemakers watch daytime television, and working people watch morning news programs and nighttime programming. In short, everyone watches television. According to him, the phenomenal number of people you can reach through television advertising makes it a bargain for your advertising dollar. So, with his advice in mind, I pursued advertising on a local television station.

I quickly discovered that television advertising, indeed, is not cheap, but it is a lot more affordable than I had imagined. Now, with cable and satellite television, there are a lot more stations with ad space to sell and often you can find "bundled" packages (three to four stations that show your commercial) that are reasonably priced for the number of households reached. This option wasn't available to me when I was starting out, so I worked with a network station sales representative to tailor a commercial that would convey my message to their targeted viewing audience.

Filming and starring in the commercial was an interesting and fun experience. I was both thrilled and proud when I saw the finished product for the first time in the studio. And when I saw *my* commercial on television, I felt my business had arrived.

Nevertheless, assessing the effect of the television ads was difficult. Was the large expenditure worth the return? And what exactly was the return on my investment? It was hard for me to measure the effectiveness of radio and television commercials because of the nature of our product. In-home pet care is not something like food or cleaning products that are needed or used daily. A pet owner may see or listen to your commercial at Thanksgiving but not need your services until the first week of July, although it was because of your November radio or television ad that they learned of your service.

While there is an implied credibility (deserved or undeserved) about businesses you see advertising on television, I think now, for the money, I would have invested in a web site for my business if the Internet had been available. For today's new pet sitter, I recommend a Yellow Pages listing, a professional-looking web site, and occasional newspaper advertising.

But the best advice I can give to today's new pet sitter is to concentrate your efforts on doing a terrific job for your clients, so they will enthusiastically tell others about your services. After all, a word-of-mouth referral is generally considered to be the best way of advertising any business.

"FREE" ADVERTISING

There are even more ways to get the word out about your business that don't require you to buy actual ad space. Mostly these are things you can do with your brochures and business cards. Here are just a few of them. Take advantage of all free opportunities to inform the public about your pet-sitting business and suggest that your staff members do the same.

● **Get involved.** Whether it's a cancer walk, your local humane society, or another charity, get involved. Represent your company by participating in your community. Not only will you benefit personally, but you will also get the word out about your business to those with whom you serve. (See chapter 6 for more about public relations.)

● **Business meetings, seminars, lectures.** Seek out resources that are available in your community for the business owner. There are often lectures and workshops sponsored by the chamber of commerce, Small Business Administration, Internal Revenue Service, or by professional groups that will help you in various aspects of running your business. These are sometimes free or offered at a nominal charge. They provide a learning experience and are valuable networking sessions. You meet others in the business world and at the same time get the opportunity to tell them about your pet-sitting service.

● **Church or synagogue activities.** Don't forget that socials, committee meetings, and circle groups consist of people who'll welcome the news of your pet-sitting services. Inform your congregation about your new business and ask for their support.

● **News releases.** These can be worth their weight in gold with the free publicity they may generate for you. Write an informative news release about the opening of your pet-sitting service and mail it to local television programs, radio stations, and newspapers. Follow up these mailings with a phone call to determine if any of the media is interested in interviewing you about your new service from either a human interest or a business angle. If they bite and put you on the local evening news, this is valuable free advertising that most small business owners could rarely afford to pay for. Aggressively go after it. "Newspapers" on page 136 shows a sample of a news release.

● **Discounts.** As mentioned earlier, offering discounts to employee groups or customers referred to you by dog groomers, travel agents, and so on, can be a terrific form of advertising. It's especially helpful in encouraging new customers to give your service a try. Discounts can also boost business during slow periods or help get your business off the ground. Once customers have used your service and have been pleased, you know they'll become repeat customers.

● **Prepare a visual presentation.** Put together a slide show or short video presentation showing your services in action. Offer to show this

GOING TO THE MARDI GRAS?

XYZ PET SITTERS, INC.
Announces 10% off

- Feed, water and exercise your pets in the comfort of your home.

- We're Bonded and Insured

"You Can Trust Your Pet to Us"

program at Board of Realtor meetings, garden club meetings, travel fairs, and other community events and meetings. Again, if you're inexperienced or uncomfortable with public speaking, now is the time for you to put your fears aside or to overcome them for the sake of your business.

● **Pleased customers.** The best form of advertising your business can have is the client who praises your services. Sometimes a service business can be slower in growing because it often depends on word-of-mouth recommendations to increase clientele and sales. Although word-of-mouth advertising may take longer to produce growth for your business, it's still the greatest advertising around. To motivate clients to tell others about your business, try offering a discount or gift certificate on future services for each referral they send you. At the very least, send a thank you note for their recommendation.

● **Open your eyes.** Watch not only for bulletin boards but also for pets in cars with their owners. Keep your business cards and brochures with you at all times—you never know when you may need one. If I saw a pet waiting in a car for his owner, I slipped a brochure under the car's windshield wiper. If I saw a pet owner out walking a dog, I stopped and asked if they had heard of our pet-sitting service. Yes, some assertiveness is necessary to run a successful business. One of my ingenious pet sitters even started studying the shopping carts in line with her at the grocery store. If she spotted pet food in the cart, she struck up a conversation with the person in line and told them about our services.

● **Look for promotion and new-hire announcements.** These appear in your local newspaper or business publications and newsletters. Send these folks one of your brochures and business cards, along with a personal note either congratulating their achievement or welcoming them to your community. End your note by saying you hope that they'll call if you can be of service to them during business or pleasure travel.

● **Public service announcements.** Many radio and television stations run a list or make announcements of the businesses that will either be open or closed for business during bad weather. Some pet-sitting firms take advantage of this to announce that their service will be open—because pet sitters, like postal carriers, usually make rounds during rain, sleet, snow, or sun. This public announcement advertises the firm's name as well as assuring and impressing the public that pets are cared for during bad weather.

● **Seize all free opportunities.** Don't forget opportunities arising at cocktail parties, PTA meetings, diet groups, exercise classes, holiday parades, craft shows, bowling leagues, day-care centers—whatever you (and your pet sitters) do when you're not actually working in your pet-sitting business. I am always stressing to new pet sitters the importance of taking advantage of all opportunities to educate others about our valuable services.

Clever Pet Sitters

I love the following advertising stories shared with me by some ingenious pet sitters.

● A pet-sitting couple was hired to care for a dog whose owners said their dog loved to listen to classical music. The owners requested that the radio be left on a classical music station during their absence, for the dog's enjoyment. The pet sitters wrote to the radio station, informing them of their four-legged fan. Loving the story, the radio station called the pet sitters and ended up doing an hour-long interview with them about their pet-sitting service, interspersed with music that had animal-related titles. Needless to say, this was invaluable advertising that resulted in several new clients for the astute pet sitters.

● One pet sitter's wife is a dental hygienist. Her work room is filled with pictures of their animals, which usually elicits comments or questions from patients. This gives her the perfect opportunity to subtly bring up the fact that her husband is a pet sitter . . . and then she launches into telling the patient about her husband's business while cleaning their teeth. The patient is a captive audience who is often unaware that such a service is available in the community. Voilà—a new customer for her husband!

• Another clever pet sitter always makes a pledge when PBS has their on-air fundraising campaign. She gives the donation from her company and challenges other pet sitters and pet lovers to match her gift.

MORE GREAT ADVERTISING IDEAS FROM READERS

In the appendix, I ask readers to write to me and share things that help their pet-sitting businesses to be successful. The pet-sitting industry is very fortunate to have such caring and dedicated members who take the time to write and share ideas, tips, and suggestions. Here are some advertising ideas offered by previous readers of this book.

• Advertise on hospital bulletin boards, because people with broken legs or recent surgeries can't walk their dog.

• Always carry business cards with you when walking a dog. Conversations always strike up with other dog owners out walking, and business cards come in handy.

• Be sure to place business cards and brochures in area feed stores.

• Whenever you leave a tip at a restaurant, leave a business card— especially if you're a generous tipper!

• Give out business cards to those with whom you do business, such as the dry cleaner, pharmacy, repair shop, barber, bank, grocery store, doctor's office, dentist, hairdresser, and so on. Tell them how much you'll appreciate them telling one person about your services.

• When you're paying your local bills by mail, enclose a business card for the accounts receivable person.

• Stick a business card in any library books that you return. Whoever next checks the book out may be a pet owner, or know someone who is.

Tip

Some great sources from which to rent mailing lists for direct mail campaigns are alumni groups, PTA memberships, church or synagogue memberships, country club memberships, and private school students.

Advertising ideas that worked well for some pet sitters and not at all for others, according to my mail, include the following:

- Ads on plastic phone book covers

- Val-Pak (direct mail) coupons

- Movie theater advertisements

- Ads on the back of grocery store receipts

Many thanks to the readers who submitted these ideas. Although I can't personally credit each submission, you know who you are! Your suggestions are appreciated, and help make the road to success much easier for new pet sitters. If you're a new pet sitter who has learned something from these tips, then pass another tip along to help someone else reading a future edition of this book.

Chapter 6

Public Relations

If running your own business is new to you, you may not be aware of what public relations is and how important it can be to your business. There is a difference between advertising and public relations, although it can sometimes seem like a fine line between the two. Both result in exposure and a positive (you hope!) public image. The difference is that advertising is normally considered to be a paid announcement; the promotion that comes from public relations is typically free media exposure.

Webster's New World Dictionary defines public relations as "relations with the general public as through publicity; specifically those functions of a corporation, organization, etc., concerned with attempting to create favorable public opinion for itself." Public relations can be a very credible—and inexpensive—way of communicating to the public the benefits and features of in-home pet-care services. As a professional pet sitter, there are many community activities you can become involved in that will demonstrate your civic spirit and increase your personal visibility. This visibility means business that can directly affect your company's bottom line.

Whether you choose to volunteer at your local Humane Society, deliver Meals on Wheels, or sponsor a Little League team, you accomplish several things for your business.

● You show your concern for the town or city in which you live. Those who participate with you may decide to do business with you because of your involvement.

● You derive personal satisfaction from your goodwill efforts.

● Some form of publicity that benefits you professionally often results from the involvement.

The publicity that comes from public relations endeavors is often more valuable than what the small business owner could ever afford to buy in the way of advertising. The good public image it creates can attract attention for your business and give you an edge over your competition. Exposure from public relations activities helps establish you as an authority and a leader in your field. In addition, it helps create a desire for your pet-sitting services and adds to the public's confidence in them.

Besides involvement with animal-related programs, such as pet therapy visits to nursing homes or hospitals, or business-related activities, such as serving on the membership committee of your local chamber of commerce, there are several other public relations options that may be of interest to you. Some of them are discussed in this chapter.

A NEWSLETTER OR E-ZINE

Consider producing a monthly, quarterly, or semiannual newsletter or e-zine (online magazine or newsletter) for your business. Sending out a company newsletter is an effective way of advertising and it's a great public relations tool. A newsletter enables you to communicate with your clients and provide them with useful information, thereby lending credibility and sincerity to your business endeavors.

In the company newsletters I produced, I always used the same design and format. This saved time and money because I didn't have to create each newsletter anew. A familiar format also increased recognition among my customers—they didn't mistake my newsletter for junk mail.

As the business owner, I wrote a personal column to inform clients of any changes in our business or payment procedures. I also used this column to thank customers for using our services.

Each newsletter contained informative material on pet care, pet products, or pet-related organizations. Pet sitters have the opportunity to influence customers to adopt healthful practices for their pets and to educate them about the latest in products, foods, toys, and so on. Your newsletter can be a wonderful way to educate your clients—but of course, first you must educate yourself. Another idea is to invite local veterinarians to provide short articles on topics of interest to pet owners. Many veterinarians will do this free of charge or for a small fee because of their commitment to the welfare of animals.

Other typical columns I usually included in my newsletters were:

● **Sitter profiles.** A brief introduction to a couple of pet sitters, their sitting routes, hobbies or special interests, and the type of pets they own or specialize in.

● **Seasonal tips.** Hot- or cold-weather concerns for pets, holiday hazards, and so on.

● **Customer profile.** This would appear if a client took an exotic trip or had an interesting job or hobby—clients love the fame of being profiled!

● **Interesting vacation destinations.** A local travel agent provided this column in exchange for an ad in the newsletter.

● **Pet-sitting stories and anecdotes.** Share an experience that has happened to you or a staff pet sitter. Humorous stories and anecdotes are entertaining, while serious stories often contain a lesson or send a message to the reader.

● **Pet-related cartoon or joke.** If you aren't artistic, hire a graphic arts student or freelancer to do a cartoon. Please don't use any cartoons from newspapers or magazines without receiving written permission from the cartoonist or publisher. And make sure any jokes or cartoons you include are not offensive to your readers.

● **Industry news.** Announcement of the PSI "Pet Sitter of the Year" contest, Professional Pet Sitters Week observances, and so on.

● **Thank yous.** Thank businesses who display your brochure or newsletter in their office, as this mention advertises their name and may make them more likely to continue to keep your materials on display. Also thank clients who have referred customers to you.

● **Congratulations.** Wish happy birthday to clients and their pets whose birthdays fall during the dates of your newsletter.

● **Schedules.** Announce office closings for holidays or special occasions.

It's best to stay away from controversial subjects in your newsletter that may offend some customers. Although it can be tempting to use it as a sounding board, it's wise to keep things light, interesting, and entertaining.

Your newsletter provides a service of offering useful information to your clients, but you can and should use it to generate business as well. Take advantage of it to announce special promotions, publish discount coupons, or even advertise for staff. (Some of your customers may be interested in pet sitting or know someone who is looking for part-time work.)

Printing a newsletter is relatively inexpensive. If you have a computer, there are many publishing software programs available that can make easy work of designing a newsletter. But even having it done by a print shop is affordable, especially if you shop around. The largest expense will be the postage for mailing the newsletter. If you plan a frequent mailing schedule, you should consider obtaining a bulk-mail permit from your post office. The permit will greatly decrease your postage costs with mass mailings. Or explore the possibility of having a mailing house handle your bulk mailings. They usually have a bulk permit available for use by customers. Of course, if you're able to do e-zines or e-blasts of your newsletter to customers, it's really inexpensive to produce.

Many pet sitters offset the costs of production by selling advertising space. By offering even a few business card–size ads, you'll help the newsletter pay for itself. With a few more ads, your newsletter could become profitable. Veterinarians, groomers, pet stores, travel agents, housecleaning and lawn-care services, home security systems, and your clients who have a product or service may be interested in advertising to your clientele.

Your newsletters (crossing that fine line between public relations and advertising) can be great advertisements for your business. Keep a supply on hand and mail one out with your brochure to potential clients who request information about your services. They can also be left in the waiting rooms of veterinarians, and doctor and dentist offices (make sure you obtain permission to leave them). Advertisers (groomers, pet stores, and so on) also are likely to let you display newsletters in their places of business.

Tip

If you use any previously published material in your newsletter, make sure you obtain permission to do so. Plagiarism and copyright infringement are serious infractions of the law.

Publishing a newsletter can be one of the best things you do for your pet-sitting business. My clients told me they genuinely appreciated receiving mine. The pennies per copy it costs to produce go a long way toward showing our customers we appreciate them and are serious about pet sitting as a profession.

A reader wrote to tell me that she had implemented a "Favorite Customer Comments" column in her newsletter. This is where she reprints compliments taken from evaluation forms or excerpts from notes attached to payments. This practice shows her clientele how much their praise is appreciated—and probably encourages some clients to consider offering it. Great idea!

NEWS RELEASES

News releases, or press releases as they are sometimes called, are exactly what the name implies—they release news to the media. When the media uses your release—in a newspaper or magazine or on a radio or television broadcast—you receive invaluable publicity. News releases can be worth their weight in gold. You'll be smart to use them in your business as often as possible.

News That Is Newsworthy

In chapter 5 I discussed the advantages of using news releases in your business. Here are some instances when you should consider issuing a news release.

- The grand opening of your business

- A new hire (new pet sitter)

- A promotion

- Any new services you add, such as pet transportation or pet food delivery

- Any awards you or your staff members receive

- Your support of any community needs/projects (such as volunteer activities)

- Membership in business organizations or professional affiliations

- Completion of a pet-sitting accreditation program or educational achievement

- Attendance at a national convention

- Business anniversaries or milestones

How to Write a News Release

Guidelines for writing a news release include the following. It may be helpful to review the sample on page 152 as you read through these points. Also refer back to the "New Pet Sitting Business Opens" sample news release in chapter 5.

- Source information (name, address, phone number) appears in the upper right corner.

- The release date appears in the upper left corner.

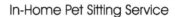

XYZ Pet Sitters, Inc.

In-Home Pet Sitting Service

Date: Contact: Amy Smith,
For: Business Name   999-8877
Release Date: Immediately   Address (or use business
NEWS RELEASE   letterhead for news release)

UNIQUE PET-SITTING SERVICE
TO CELEBRATE GRAND OPENING

Anytown, NC . . . XYZ Pet Sitters, a professional pet-sitting service, will open Monday, April 21. The only business of its type in this area, the new firm will serve pet owners throughout Forsyth county.

The unique service will provide in-home pet care as an alternative to kennels or leaving pets in the care of neighbors or friends. The company offers additional services to its clients, such as watering plants, rotating lights, bringing in mail and newspapers and generally giving the home a "lived in" look.

"Our staff will include six pet sitters who have completed a training program and are bonded and insured," says Amy Smith, president of the service agency. "Our goal is to make it much easier for Forsyth county pet owners to travel by using our quality pet-care services." XYZ Pet Sitters is also a member of Pet Sitters International, an educational organization for professional pet sitters.

Interested persons may call 999-8877 for more information or to reserve a pet sitter. XYZ Pet Sitters needs at least four days notice before a client is planning to leave town so a sitter may visit the home, become familiar with the pets, review needed services and confirm the assignment.

# # #

Member of

Bonded   123 Any Street • Anywhere, U.S.A. 20002
Insured   (909) 999-8877 • www.yourwebsite.com

• The headline summarizes the content of the release and is typed in capital letters.

• The first paragraph of the release identifies who, what, when, where, why, and how. Your headline and first paragraph often determine whether the reader (the editor) is intrigued enough to read more of your release—and use it.

• Always type a news release, double spaced, and leave wide margins.

• Keep paragraphs and sentences short and to the point.

• Usually the shorter the release, the better. However, if a longer release is needed to do the subject justice, space your text so one paragraph ends at the bottom of a page and a new paragraph begins at the top of the next page.

• On the last page, the end of the release is indicated by "-O-" or "# # #" or "END." This is normally centered under the final paragraph.

• Carefully proofread for typing or spelling errors.

• Always send a good, clean copy of your news release to the media—preferably on business letterhead.

Tip

A tremendous benefit of membership in an organization like Pet Sitters International is that professionally prepared news releases are made available for members to personalize and send to their local media. These are interesting and informative press releases that enhance your credibility on the local level and help increase the success of your business.

Compiling a Media List

Take some time to put together a local media list for your news release mailings. Include newspapers (large and small), radio stations, television stations, and area magazines. A media list may be available from your local chamber of commerce. If not, make some phone calls to find out the name of the appropriate editor or producer to whose attention the release should be sent. Sometimes the people in these positions change, so make every effort to keep your list current.

If a photograph can enhance the story behind your news release, it's a good idea to provide one with your mailing or write at the bottom of your release, "Photo available upon request" with an e-mail address for the request.

> ### *Tip*
>
> Publicity photos are best when there is action taking place, when the number of people involved is limited, and, of course, when an animal is involved. Before taking any photos of clients' pets or homes, be sure to obtain their permission.

Newspapers have their own photographers, but there are only so many subjects in a day they can cover. Sending a photograph demonstrates the visual impact of your story—even to television news people—that creates interest in generating news coverage.

After determining the number of news releases you'll need, get them in the mail early enough that you're consistent with the release date at the top of your news release. If you haven't heard from any editors or producers within a week after mailing, follow up with a phone call. Politely ask if they received the release, if they plan to use it, or if they need additional information or a photograph to accompany the article. Don't be discouraged or take it personally if an editor is brief or negative about using your news release. These people receive many news releases and news tips every day. If your first attempts with news releases don't succeed, try again. When your efforts result in free publicity, you'll see that news releases are a worthwhile investment of time and money.

PUBLIC SPEAKING

Yes, I know that speaking in public is one of people's greatest fears, because I suffer from it too! According to something I recently read, public speaking is more feared than death or divorce. However, I have found that if you can shake your way through it, public speaking is probably the best free publicity you can get for your business. The good news is that it does get easier the more you do it.

Numerous opportunities are available for guest speakers in most communities. Because people tend to do business with people they know, or are at least familiar with, public speaking engagements will greatly increase the likelihood of listeners using your services. Here are some groups you could make a presentation available to.

● **Civic clubs.** Jaycees, Kiwanis, Masons, Elks, Rotarians, and the list goes on and on. See if your local chamber of commerce has a listing of civic clubs available, along with contact information.

● **Business groups.** Chamber of commerce functions and local professional groups, such as accountants, secretaries, personnel managers, realtors, and women's networks hold regular meetings where interesting guest speakers are in demand.

• **Garden clubs.** Even if members do not have pets, they most likely know someone who does or may need their plants watered by your service during absences from home.

• **School children.** A great place to educate about responsible pet care—and the advantages of using a pet sitter. What parent can refuse a child's request to use a pet sitter?

Keep in mind that few people are born great public speakers—for most of us it takes practice, practice, practice. Write your speech on index cards and practice in front of family, friends, and coworkers. This will greatly increase your comfort level. Try to add some humor; everyone enjoys a good laugh, and it will make you and your audience more relaxed. Use visual aids when possible (overheads, the public relations video *What Is Pet Sitting?*, your brochures, and so on), and dress comfortably but businesslike.

Don't underestimate yourself! Audiences are composed of people who admire your ability to stand up in front of them and who want to hear what you have to say. You can do this! You don't have to, but believing in your business and the great service you're providing will help make the task easier. Remember that public speaking will really help your business grow.

> ### *Tip*
>
> If you ever hear me at a public speaking engagement, know that the butterflies and nervousness are there and please be kind!

EXHIBITION BOOTHS

There are many opportunities in most communities to rent booth space at all kinds of events. Although some of these are strictly advertising mediums, such as bridal fairs and travel or business expositions, others are more closely aligned to public relations, such as participating in a pet fair with veterinarians, groomers, or animal transport services, or having a booth at a local dog or cat show. Regardless of the event's location, these guidelines may be helpful to maximize the potential from a booth display.

• Other participants may be much larger companies with prefabricated booths. You'll want to make your booth display as professional as possible. Reserve a table from the promoters—these are usually skirted and look nicer.

● Find out if there is a color theme to the show so you can try to match your display materials to it.

● If electricity is available, consider having a small television with a VCR at your table. This enables you to play taped television spots about your company (if you've appeared on any local programs), pet-sitting videos, or pet first-aid/care videos.

● Use brochure and business card stands to display company literature.

● Use a fishbowl for a door-prize drawing to be held for free pet-sitting services or a giveaway item. Require names and addresses so you can mail brochures or coupons at a later date.

● Remember that food attracts people! Have a plate of animal crackers or a dish of candy for visitors. Giveaway items, such as balloons for children or magnets for adults, are also popular. Bookmarks (available from Pet Sitters International) disappear quickly.

● Buy some inexpensive picture frames to showcase collages of customer's pets, association membership documents, or your own pets. Old calendars are a good source for eye-catching photographs of pets. Stuffed animals can add visual appeal.

● Have a nice vinyl or acrylic sign made by a sign company or, if you have a computer and color printer, make some nice banners for your booth.

● Display your Client Presentation Book (see chapter 3).

● If there is a local network of pet sitters in your area, consider jointly renting booth space at exhibitions to increase exposure while holding down costs.

● Make sure you've arranged for relief help in staffing your booth, to allow you time for meals, breaks, and to walk around and meet the other exhibitors.

Besides the attending audience you'll reach with exhibition space, most shows receive coverage from local television, radio, and newspapers, which can greatly increase your exposure. Forethought and planning will result in a nice booth display that you can use again and again. Plus, it will help you enjoy yourself while promoting your business.

SPECIAL EVENTS

You may prefer to create your own public relations programs. Some ideas for you to consider include:

● **Pet photo day.** Hold an event where pet owners can bring their pet(s) for a professional photo (there are many pet photographers out there now and some who travel the country doing fundraising shoots). Donate the sitting fee to a deserving local animal-related cause.

● **Fur "ball."** Coordinate a dinner and dance where dogs and their people can both enjoy the festivities. Donate ticket proceeds to an animal-related organization.

● **Dog walkathon.** Sponsor a morning or afternoon walk at a local park. Give registration fees to an animal-related charity.

● **Halloween pet costume contest.** Sponsor a contest where pet owners can submit photographs of their pets in costume. Charge an entry fee that can be donated to a local pet charity.

● **Profit sharing.** Donate a percentage of your annual profits to a local pet shelter or charity. Indicate on your company literature that you do this and then issue a news release when you make the annual contribution.

● **Take Your Dog to Work Day.** This event takes place every June to celebrate the great companions dogs make and to encourage their adoption. Get involved through PSI or your local community.

It is the animals who benefit from special fundraisers like these, but there are benefits for the participating pet sitter as well. Doors will open to you from public relations efforts. However, it is often enough just to know you've helped make a difference.

BUSINESS ETIQUETTE

Good business etiquette is an important aspect of public relations. Remember all the people you called upon to help you build your business: the groomers, veterinarians, kennels, travel agents, hairdressers—even other pet sitters? It's a good public relations idea to go a step further and thank these folks in some way. After all, you want to stay on their good side.

Saying thanks can involve simply sending a handwritten note on a holiday card or dropping off a box of fresh doughnuts for a morning coffee break. The Christmas season provides a great opportunity to deliver a special gift to those who have contributed to your business's success. If you're too busy during this time, there's always Valentine's Day or a goodie basket for Easter.

The same etiquette applies to customers. If the length of your client list prohibits sending holiday cards to all of them, a heartfelt "thanks" in your company newsletter will suffice. For customers who allow you to use them as references or for those who send referrals to you, a gift certificate or a coupon for future pet-sitting services will be an appreciated gesture.

Pet sitting, by nature, is a very personal business with the access it provides to people's homes, pets, and lives. Practice good business etiquette so that you'll enjoy favorable public relations.

Chapter 7

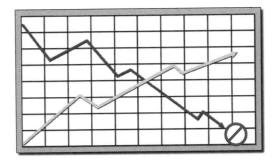

Examining the Negatives

When exploring a possible investment or career opportunity, it is important to examine the negatives. I was fortunate that I experienced very few serious problems, and the positive aspects of running and operating a pet-sitting service far outweighed the negative ones for me. I've found that most problems can be solved with a potent combination of common sense and determination; many problems can be avoided or minimized with some forethought and planning.

With that said, since the first edition of this book, many readers have asked me to address the drawbacks of pet sitting. Others have shared problems they've experienced or ones they've anticipated. This chapter is a combination of my own experiences, those readers have shared with me, and the challenges that have arisen as our industry has matured in recent years.

Pet sitters who work alone face the biggest drawback of the profession: If you don't have any employees, you may find yourself working nearly 365 days a year. Holidays are especially busy times for pet sitters, so you may find that family celebrations will have to be adjusted to fit around your schedule. Of course, these problems can be remedied or minimized by having a staff of sitters; that way, weekend and holiday assignments can be rotated. Or you can choose to operate your service only during certain months of the year, such as May to September. However, there are so many benefits to pet sitting that I found the sacrifice of working on holidays to be a small concession.

Depending on the area in which you live, weather can be a drawback to pet sitting. I'll be the first to admit that walking a dog (or several of them) on a chilly, rainy day can be less than pleasurable, as is sliding around with a dog in six inches of sleet and snow. Still, I can't think of any job that comes without imperfections, can you? When it was a gorgeous spring day and I was out

> ### Tip
>
> If you plan to work alone, remember that a reputable pet sitter should make provisions for backup services. Doing so will give you and your clients peace of mind if, for whatever reason, you are not able to personally make visits as contracted.

walking those same dogs—well, it was hard to believe I would actually get paid for having so much fun and getting some exercise, too.

The emotional attachments you develop with your clientele can be a negative of this profession, especially if you happen to be tender hearted. Since we often become just like one of the family, it's easy to develop loving relationships with animals that will leave you as heartbroken and upset as the owner is when a pet dies. (The upside to this, of course, is all the love you've received and known from the pet.)

A minor drawback to pet sitting is that you can expect to hear occasional criticism of your fees. When setting your prices, you'll probably find that your fees are higher than the local boarding kennel's (unless the assignment involves multiple pets—then a pet sitter is usually less expensive than a kennel). While we are living in an age of pet indulgence, there are still some pet owners who are not accustomed to spending much on their pets, whether it's for veterinary care, diet, or the TLC you'll be providing. You just have to take this infrequent objection in stride and realize that you provide a specialized service that not everyone is going to appreciate or use. Fortunately, many pet owners think the world of their pets and will gladly pay your fees—which are actually reasonable considering the peace of mind your service affords them when they are away from home. My experience was that for every person who complained that my fees were too high, there were probably five who asked, "Is that all you charge?"

Burnout can also be a problem. Although no profession is immune, a pet sitter (especially one who works alone) really has to guard against it. Caring for pets can be so enjoyable that you may find yourself having a hard time telling clients no or "I'm already booked for next weekend." Not wanting to disappoint a client or lose out on the business, you'll find yourself taking on too much and running yourself ragged. Exhaustion soon leads to burnout. If you rarely have time off or continually miss out on holiday celebrations, you'll find burnout occurring sooner rather than later. By recognizing that this threat exists, you'll be able to structure your staff accordingly and schedule reservations wisely to prevent burnout from ruining what can be a wonderful career. The best advice I can give you as a new pet sitter starting out is to control your business *from the start* rather than letting it (or your customers) control you. For many of us to successfully do this, we first must learn how to say no.

JUST SAY NO

One little word. How can it be so hard to say? Is there something peculiar to the pet-sitting profession that makes saying no an impossible feat?

Are we so afraid that if we don't accept every last-minute reservation or sit for the client with the nasty, filthy home, our business will be doomed to failure? Is it because we're an industry dominated by women or because we're just plain old nice folks that *no* doesn't seem to belong in our vocabularies? Whatever the cause, it has become obvious that this is an industry-wide problem with which pet sitters must come to terms. Your business success—and your sanity—rely heavily on being able to say, simply and confidently, no.

Eventually, it will happen. You'll be completely booked for the weekend, or maybe you blocked the weekend out for some much-needed time off. At about 9 p.m. on Friday evening, the phone will ring with a customer begging you for weekend services. You will sigh and accept the job, even though it will really stretch you or will mean giving up the time off you'd planned—and you'll hate yourself for not saying no!

Or maybe a customer will complain that your prices are too high and try to get you to lower your fees. You'll hesitate as you think how, on occasion, you feel a little guilty about charging what you do for fun, "easy" jobs . . . and this is a beautiful home to visit . . . and maybe you could knock a little off your fee. . . .

Or perhaps the client will acknowledge on the phone that her dog is territorial and has been known to act aggressively toward strangers. But she'll dismiss these actions with the comment, "If you're a pet-care professional, you won't have any problem." Before you realize it, you've agreed to set up an initial meeting and dread the situation already.

And then there's the client whose address is in a less than desirable neighborhood where you're not comfortable making rounds, yet you hate to turn away business. Stop!

If there's one thing I learned in my many years of pet sitting, it's to listen to my gut feelings, my instincts, that inner voice, the little radar—and just say no.

Think about it. One of the benefits of owning your own business is that you have the power and the right to say no. You are your own boss and you dictate when, how, and for whom you work. Just because you serve the public doesn't mean you have to serve all the people all the time. Pet-sitting services are not suitable for all (for example, people with aggressive dogs or filthy homes). Even Sears closes its doors occasionally! It has hours when you can shop or call the store and hours when you cannot. Most businesses and professions have rules—policies and procedures—that enable them to operate efficiently and effectively.

As professional pet sitters, we need to make a concerted effort not to sell ourselves short; we must demand to be treated as the professional business people we are. People will take advantage of you—but only if you let them. So how do you learn to say no? Here are some suggestions for going about it in a tactful manner.

• **The last-minute caller.** Deter these calls by adding a last-minute-reservation surcharge to your fees. If you're going to accommodate these inconvenient and sometimes inconsiderate customers, make it worth your time! Besides, when you hit the customer in the pocketbook, they often get the message. If you do not want to accept a last-minute job, simply explain that you're completely booked for that time period. To accept any more assignments would decrease the amount of time you have contracted for previously scheduled clients. Tell the client that you're sure they can appreciate your position and that you hope they will call you again in the future—but with a little more advance notice! There's nothing wrong with being completely booked—it shows that your services are in demand. And even if you're not booked, this excuse provides a tactful reason to politely say no.

• **The after-hours caller.** Especially if your office is in your home, establish certain office hours for calls and reservations and then stick to them. When it's not office hours, turn the ringer off on your telephone and the sound down on your answering machine. If you accept calls at all hours of the day and night, people will call you at all hours. If you set specific times for calls and announce them to your customers, they will soon adjust and abide by these hours (except in emergencies). You must set the rules for your business—and for your customers. Also, if you are completely booked for a weekend (whether it's working or taking time off!), let your answering machine announce this to possible last-minute callers and say that calls for future services will be returned during your next scheduled office hours.

• **The client who tries to get you to come down on your fees or to give them a discount on multiple visits.** Do they ask their doctor for a reduced fee? Does the grocer or gas station give them a break at the cash register because they've shopped there several times that week? No—and neither should you! Politely explain that you are a professional pet sitter and, as such, there is more than meets the eye to your services. There are the hidden costs of insurance, bonding, advertising, office overhead, taxes, printing, supplies, gas, and so on that the client tends to overlook. All the client sees is the visit to their home. When you stand your ground and firmly but tactfully explain this, and how professionally your service is operated, the client should respect your prices. If they don't, remember that your services are not for everyone. As soon as you give a price break, this will turn out to be the job from hell.

Sure, some assignments are easier than others—but for every easy assignment, there are two more where the fee should be doubled!

- **The client with the aggressive dog.** It's very easy to explain that your company policy prohibits you from sitting for pets who have bitten anyone or acted aggressively in the past. Say that you'll be happy to give the caller some names and numbers of area kennels; or say that the caller might prefer to ask a family member who is familiar with the dog to provide care. End the call by saying "I'm sorry I can't help you, but thank you for calling."

- **The client in the crime-ridden neighborhood.** Simply explain that you don't provide pet-sitting services in that zip code, or the western part of town, or whatever. Explain that you haven't received enough interest in services from that neighborhood to make it worthwhile to expand your sitting territory to the area. You could offer to take the client's name and number, saying that if you start a service route in their neighborhood, you will let them know. Don't forget that it's your choice where you pet sit, and this is a diplomatic way of saying no.

- **The client with the nasty, filthy home.** This situation can be a little more awkward, because you normally won't know the condition of the home until you're actually there for the initial interview. If you are uncomfortable with the assignment after seeing the interior of a home, explain that you don't feel comfortable accepting the assignment and would prefer that the customer make other arrangements for pet care. If you're not brave enough to say no while you're face to face with a client, call them immediately upon leaving to explain that you gave it some thought while driving home and decided it would be better if they made other arrangements for pet care because you don't feel comfortable with the living/working conditions of the home, then promptly return the house key if you accepted one at the initial interview. Sure, the client may be angry or upset at personal criticism of their housekeeping, but better that than a miserable pet-sitting assignment for you. We can't please everyone, and the sooner we learn this lesson, the smarter we'll be. (Another out for this situation was shared by a pet-sitting colleague. She simply calls the client after leaving the home and explains that she has just realized she has a conflict with the dates involved that will prevent her from accepting the job.)

- **The client who requests extra services, late-night visits, or something above and beyond your typical services.** Explaining that lawn mowing or housecleaning is not a part of your business should suffice (you can't blame a person for asking!). The client will likely appreciate a referral to these types of services. If you are willing to make an exception and mow the lawn or run

A Filthy Home

I had a client who, even though she had a master's degree and was a professional in the community, was an extremely poor housekeeper. Boxes of junk were piled from floor to ceiling in several rooms of her house, clothes were everywhere except the closets, and the cats—who probably tired of a seldom-clean litter box—used other parts of the home for their bathroom facilities. As you might imagine, the situation was very unpleasant. The pet sitter assigned to the client was a real cat lover, however, and she felt her visits were the only times these cats were properly cared for and attended to. She opted to wear a face mask to the home (which was, in essence, a large litter box) and sat for this slovenly pet owner for several years. Finally, the client was transferred. We always wondered how in the world she sold her house!

an errand for a customer, again, make it worth your time. My experience has shown that customers are so glad you're willing to accommodate their special needs that they will gladly pay your asking price. And most people know when they're asking for something above and beyond your normal services. Remember that people can't take advantage of you unless you let them.

• **The client who criticizes your services and refuses to pay.** If you pet sit long enough, you're bound to run into this customer eventually. Regardless of the lengths you went to during the assignment, they are determined that you are at fault and they shouldn't have to pay. A personal note here: I consider myself to be among the most honest, ethical, and fair people around. If I was at fault, or if I thought my pet sitter was wrong, I readily admitted it and attempted to make amends with the client. If I thought my pet sitter or I did everything humanly possible to fulfill our contract with a client, however, I fought to the bitter end. In other words, once in while I had to say, "No, we won't accept your complaints and allegations, and we expect our bill to be paid." And I stood by that, even if it meant going to small claims court to settle the matter (see chapter 3). Some people and businesses adhere to the philosophy that the customer is always right. I have learned that this is not always the case in pet sitting. The customer has the right to have an opinion or to try to get out of paying their bill, but that doesn't make them right!

I hope you'll learn, sooner instead of later, that it is okay to say no. Standing up for ourselves and our established business policies and practices will create respect and solidify the professionalism we're creating and commanding for our industry. It will also help you build confidence in yourself and your abilities. Plus, it will preserve your sanity and keep pet sitting a career you enjoy.

Some Tips to Avoid Burnout

- Try to work eight-hour days.

- Schedule time off for yourself and put it on your calendar, just as if it is a pet-sitting interview or assignment.

- Plan weekends off and vacation time. Announce these times you will be unavailable to customers via your answering machine and newsletters. If clients have advance notice of your unavailability, they'll often try to schedule their travel around your calendar.

- Set office hours for taking and returning phone calls or e-mails, and stick to them!

- Plan to attend the annual conventions of Pet Sitters International. They enable you to learn things that will help you business-wise and also help you recharge your batteries. They are usually held at a location that can be combined with a vacation and are announced a year in advance, so clients and you can plan in advance. Remember that sometimes the best thing you can do for your business is to get away from it!

INDUSTRY CHALLENGES

As the pet-sitting industry has evolved, some important issues have affected it. While I'm sure the future may hold additional challenges that have not even occurred to us to think about yet, I want to give you the heads up on these. These stories are shared to educate you, not to scare you about the career you're considering. Better to be forewarned and forearmed when it comes to avoiding or handling problems.

State Veterinary Boards

The first issue involves pet sitters who give prescription medicine to pets under their care. The State of Ohio Veterinary Board recently challenged this practice by some Ohio pet sitters, alleging they were practicing veterinary medicine without a license. As you might expect, giving previously prescribed medications to pets under our care has been standard industry practice for years. Many pet owners would not be able to leave home were it not for professional pet sitters who are willing to provide this necessary and valuable service.

The Ohio pet sitters were able to resolve the dispute with the Ohio Veterinary Board, but it would be a good idea to read the rules and regulations as set forth by the veterinary board of your state. If your state laws read that medicines may be administered by "someone acting as an agent of the pet's owner," then pet sitters have every right to offer this service. If they read otherwise, it would be a good idea to start getting written authorization from the pet's owner to administer any medications and to ask your client to have the authorization signed by their veterinarian.

The second situation involves those pet sitters who are also registered veterinary technicians (RVT). According to what an RVT pet sitter in California recently learned, an RVT cannot independently operate a pet health-care service or advertise and promote the service of administering medications, because anything a RVT does *must be under the supervision of a veterinarian*. While an RVT license is active, they are under the jurisdiction of the state veterinary medical board. If you hold a Registered Veterinary Technician license and are seriously considering pet sitting as a profession, I encourage you to check your state laws to find out what you can and cannot do as a professional pet sitter.

With the size and continued growth of the pet-sitting industry, it's to be expected that we'll occasionally be challenged. My understanding is that groomers, pet massage therapists, and others in pet-related fields have had their doors knocked on, too, by state veterinary boards. The veterinary industry is only trying to protect their livelihood, so to some extent, you can't blame them. It's my hope, though, that the veterinary industry will realize that professional pet sitters are only trying to make the lives of pet owners easier.

It has never been our intention to diagnose or prescribe treatments or in any way attempt to practice veterinary medicine. However, it is often the observant pet sitter who notices a change in the pet's behavior that leads to a veterinary visit. And it's often the pet sitter who refers clients who are new to the community to local veterinarians for their pet's health-care needs. Reciprocally, many vets who don't provide boarding services or whose kennels may be full will recommend pet sitters to their clientele. It's a win-win-win for pets, people, and vets when our industries work together.

Internal Revenue Audits for Use of Independent Contractors

It has been industry practice to use independent contractors, for several reasons. The split-shift hours involved with morning and evening visits, the seasonal nature of busier times, and the tendency for some pet sitters to specialize in a particular breed or species' care (cats, birds, horses) can mean sporadic periods of work. Thus, it can be more cost effective for businesses to use pet sitters as independent contractors rather than full- or part-time employees.

Using independent contractors legally involves meeting what's referred to as the IRS's Common Law Factors (formally Twenty Common Law Factors or, informally, 20 Questions test). Being able to use independent contractors means that you, as an employer, don't have to withhold or match any state or federal payroll taxes. Since this means less revenue for the government, you can understand why the IRS takes a hard look at businesses using independent contractors to make sure they are meeting the Common Law Factors.

This wouldn't be a problem if it weren't for the fact that the IRS factors are not exactly clear. Since they are a little fuzzy, you may interpret the rule one way and the IRS may see it another way. Couple this with the fact that each state has different laws regarding the use of independent contractors and it gets even more confusing about if and how independent contractors can be used in a business. And if the IRS or your state challenges your use of independent contractors, they most likely aren't going to be disposed to seeing things your way.

That's not to say that a pet-sitting business can't be run using independent contractors—it can. I successfully used them in my pet-sitting business, but I was also never audited. Pet-sitting businesses of which I am aware who have been audited have gone both ways—some won their case and ability to use independent contractors and others were forced to change to an employer/employee relationship but given "safe haven" for past payroll taxes not paid.

The difference in whether a business won or lost their case for independent contractors most likely stemmed from the fact that while there has been steady use of independent contractors in this industry, there has not been a *consistent practice* in the way they are used. For example, some business owners have the client pay the independent contractor for the assignment and then the independent contractor pays the pet-sitting service a referral fee for the job. Other firms collect payment from the client and then pay the independent contractor a contracted commission. Both methods may be acceptable ways to operate with independent contractors; this is only an example to show you that there are myriad ways pet-sitting businesses operate in using them.

Until our industry is able to obtain a ruling on the use of independent contractors similar to one the National Association of Realtors (NAR) secured—which specifies how independent contractors must be treated industry-wide—individual pet-sitting businesses need to carefully discuss the advantages and disadvantages of employees versus independent contractors with their accountants and attorneys. Learn as much as you can about these staffing options for your business so you can make the choice you're most comfortable with in operating your business.

Do I think the pet-sitting industry will be able to lobby the IRS for a ruling on independent contractors in the near future? It's through trade organizations like Pet Sitters International and the NAR that these movements are often spearheaded. The NAR is the largest trade association in the United States, with more than one million members. Since it takes large numbers of members and lots of money for these efforts, my guess is that since PSI has 7,400 members as of this writing, we still have a way to go before trying for a favorable outcome with the IRS.

Dog Bites

According to the news media, it seems that dog bites have been increasing in recent years. Within our industry, it's not that pet sitters are being bitten more frequently, it's that other people (third parties) are being bitten (or injured) more often by dogs who are under a pet sitter's care. If that happens, it's your responsibility. Needless to say, this is not something you want to experience. So, to be on the safe side, here are some suggestions.

Find out as much as you can about a dog's temperament. Ask the owner if the dog has ever bitten a human or another animal. Find out if he is neutered. Ask about how he reacts to the owner's absence from home: Is he territorial or would he lick a burglar to death? How does the dog act toward children? Has he been obedience trained and what commands does he know? Is he leash trained?

If you're uncomfortable with the answers to any of these questions and you would be expected to walk or exercise this dog in a public place, my advice is to turn down the assignment. Dog bites are painful, traumatic, and can be expensive, to say the least. Why take the risk when there are so many good, sweet dogs out there?

If you are out walking a dog (on leash, of course) and anyone tries to approach the dog, don't let them. People have good intentions but again, it's too big a risk to take while the dog is in your care and under your control. Ask them not to approach. This may be the gentlest dog ever, but you never know when something may frighten him and spark the instinct to bite. While a dog owner's homeowners insurance may cover dog-bite-injury expenses that occur on the pet/homeowner's property, any expenses resulting while the dog is in your care, custody, and control are your responsibility.

Speaking of homeowner's insurance, some insurers are taking steps to minimize their exposure to dog-bite claims. Some companies are asking dog owners to sign liability waivers for dog bites, while others charge more for specific breeds such as Rottweilers and Akitas. Other insurance companies are excluding certain breeds from coverage, while still others will exclude a dog from coverage once he is known to have bitten. This may be something you want to discuss with your client, depending upon any concerns you have about their dog's temperament and what your company policy is regarding liability for any injuries sustained from their dog.

Off-Leash Dog Parks

When these first became available, dog owners and pet sitters (along with the dogs) jumped for joy. Now that they have become much more prevalent and we've all had a chance to see how they work, problems have surfaced. It's not the ideal venue for every dog.

I think most pet sitters agree that off-leash parks are just fine when the owner wants to take their dog there. But when the pet sitter is in charge, there's too much risk involved with fights between other dogs and with dogs having easy access to people. In other words, to best control the actions of dogs under your care, keep them leashed.

Demanding Clientele

With pets being considered as true family members and surrogate children for many pet owners today, the standards for pet care have been raised. This is not only true of expectations of professional pet sitters; you can see it in the transformations that have taken place in the boarding kennel industry in recent years. Kennels have gone upscale with rooms for pets that contain televisions or piped-in music, and many offer spa services or planned activities for their charges. These changes were due to the anthropomorphic thinking of today's pet owner, who is demanding quality care on par with what they themselves might expect.

This, coupled with the fact that the pet-sitting industry is growing fast, means today's pet sitter must stay on the cutting edge to remain competitive. Credentials such as industry accreditation programs and pet first-aid training are becoming more important indicators of professionalism, and this trend will most likely grow in the future. Staying current on pet-related issues, pet-care practices, and business trends in pet sitting will contribute to your success in meeting the sophisticated needs of today's pet-owning population. This can be achieved, in part, by reading pet and trade journals, networking with other pet sitters, and keeping an active membership with an industry association.

DON'T DO THIS!

You've already learned that to be a truly professional pet sitter, you need to carry business liability insurance. If you're not totally convinced by now, I hope you will be after reading this section.

Now that a specialized pet sitter's liability insurance policy has been available for more than ten years, we have a claims history for our industry. You can benefit by knowing about claims that have been filed and taking steps to guard against these problems in your own pet-sitting business.

Insurance is something we hope we never have to use, but sometimes there are legitimate situations where you, and your clients, are glad you have reputable coverage in place. Then again, there are some claims where you wonder if this pet sitter should even be in business! For your contemplation and education, here are some actual claims filed by pet sitters in recent years, and the amount of money the insurance company paid out. Please keep in mind as you read these that my intent is not to frighten you away from pet sitting, but to help you avoid problems others have encountered.

● While an insured pet sitter was putting leashes on a client's dogs, the dogs got tangled up. In the ensuing confusion, the pet sitter knocked a lamp into the client's laptop computer, breaking the screen. Paid: $1,372.

● A dog whom an insured pet sitter was taking care of got into a package of rat poison, so pet sitter took the dog to the vet to be treated. Paid: $414.87.

● An insured pet sitter was taking care of a puppy and when he put the dog back into the crate, he did not latch it correctly. The puppy got out, then found and chewed up a pen, which got ink all over the client's carpet. Paid: $938.88.

● While an insured pet sitter was walking a client's dog, she noticed that he began to limp and whimper. She took the dog to the vet, where he was treated for a torn ligament. Paid: $1,154.82.

● An insured pet sitter accidentally left the water on in one of the sinks in a client's home. The water overflowed and damaged the client's laundry room and pantry. Paid: $980.95.

● An insured pet sitter was watching three dogs and was to water the Christmas tree while there. The water overflowed from the Christmas tree into the carpet and stained the carpet. Paid: $1,028.86.

> ### *Tip*
>
> Watch that water! Especially when watering a client's plants, don't let it overflow onto the furniture.

● An insured pet sitter was playing with a client's dog, and the dog ingested a small rubber spatula. The dog was taken to the vet, who performed an endoscopy to remove the spatula. Paid: $823.

● A client left instructions for her two cats to stay in a particular bedroom. When the insured pet sitter arrived at the home, she found the cats out in the middle of the house. She assumed that since there was no damage, it would be fine to allow the cats to stay out. Unfortunately, she was wrong, and the cats tore up two oriental rugs. Paid: $746.

● An insured pet sitter put up a gate to keep a client's dog in part of the home. The client had advised the pet sitter against trying this. The dog chewed the carpet and the padding trying to get around the gate. Paid: $925.

> ### *Tip*
>
> Follow your client's instructions! Have a checklist if you need one.

● An insured pet sitter was taking care of two dogs at a client's home. She was instructed to leave the air conditioner on. Upon return, the client found her Pug near death. Her dog had suffered from heat stroke because the pet sitter did not leave the air on as instructed. Paid: $192.

● An insured pet sitter tried to open a client's garage door to get to the dog food. The door was caught on a container in the garage, but the pet sitter did not realize this and continued to open the door. This bent the metal panels and the arms that raise the door, which had to be replaced. Paid: $510.

● An insured pet sitter was walking two dogs using a double leash. When leaving the park, the pet sitter lost her grip on the leash. Both dogs went in opposite directions and the leash tripped a nearby pedestrian, who sustained bodily injury. Paid: $115,000.

● An insured pet sitter dropped sugar on a client's throw rug. When she went to shake the rug out, she hit the bar and broke four wine glasses. Paid: $189.

● A cat urinated on a hardwood floor several times, and the insured pet sitter failed to clean it up. As a result, the flooring had to be replaced. Paid: $3,099.

● An insured pet sitter was using nail polish and spilled it on the client's table. When trying to clean up the mess, the table was severely damaged. Paid: $4,106.

● An insured pet sitter was taking care of a client's dog. The dog had a bowel movement in the house. She cleaned it up and disposed of it in the upstairs bathroom. The toilet clogged and overflowed, causing extensive damage to the house. Paid: $5,790.63.

● While an insured pet sitter was walking a dog, she lost her ring of keys. The client had to change their locks and replace twenty keys. Paid: $345.50.

● While an insured pet sitter was walking a dog, the animal stepped into glass and cut his front left paw. The dog was taken to vet to be treated. Paid: $478.75.

● An insured pet sitter was walking two dogs when a Rottweiler came out and attacked them, injuring both the dogs in the pet sitter's care. This claim was denied by the insurance company because the pet sitter was not negligent, the owner of the Rottweiler was. However, the pet sitter forgot to get the name of the Rottweiler's owner, so the sitter ended up having to pay for the injuries. Always get the name (and contact information) of the other party any time an accident occurs! Also, even if you think you may not be at fault, always turn in a potential claim immediately to your insurance company.

● While in an insured pet sitter's care, a dog slipped out of his collar and was hit by a car. Paid: $3,977.

● An insured pet sitter did not close a closet door, and the client's dog ingested medication that was in closet. The pet was taken to the vet for treatment. Paid: $957.

● An insured pet sitter opened a sliding glass door in a client's home, and the dog jumped onto the screen door, knocking it off its track and breaking the frame. Paid: $204.

● An insured pet sitter was cleaning a client's frog tank and set the light (on an automatic timer) on the floor. She forgot to put it back on the tank, and it burned the carpet. Paid: $1,915.

- An insured pet sitter took a child she was providing childcare for to a client's home, where the dog she was pet sitting for bit the child. Paid: $5,000.

- An insured pet sitter took a client's dog for a walk. The dog walked through tar and then tracked it through the house and onto the furniture. Paid: $9,266.

- An insured pet sitter had taken a client's dog off the leash while in his care. The dog got a cut on her right paw while running. Paid: $453.

- An insured pet sitter forgot to visit a client's home as promised. The cat urinated on a leather sofa. Fortunately, the missed visit caused no harm to the cat—but the sofa had to be replaced. Paid $904.32.

- An insured pet sitter closed the door upon leaving a client's home and heard the dog yelp. She noticed blood on the floor and the dog's tail underneath the door. The dog was taken to the vet and four inches of tail had to be amputated. Paid: $605.24.

- When caring for a fishpond, an insured pet sitter removed the wrong filter and the pond drained, killing twenty imported fish. Paid: $2,543.

- An insured pet sitter was walking a client's dog on a bike path. As a woman on roller blades went to pass, the dog bit her on the arm. Paid: $15,000.

- An insured pet sitter was walking a dog through an apartment complex. The dog bit a passerby on the knee. Paid: $12,000.

Tip

Please be sure to use extreme caution when walking dogs around other people, especially children, as they are the most frequent victims of dog bites. When strangers, no matter how friendly they appear, approach you and the dog you are walking, be aware that just warning them to stay away from the dog does not relieve you from liability. You are responsible for keeping the dog from biting anyone or anything while that dog is in your care. If you have pet sitters on staff, please educate them about this fact and about how to avoid confrontations.

● An insured pet sitter was taking care of an outdoor fishpond. One of her duties was to monitor and maintain the water level in the pond. After filling the pond, the pet sitter left the water on by mistake and killed all the fish. Paid: $500.

● An insured pet sitter was taking care of a dog who had a foot injury. (This was a previous injury and had nothing to do with the claim.) The pet sitter decided to give the dog an aspirin to help with the pain. The owners had not left instructions nor given permission for the pet sitter to do so. The dog had a bad reaction to the medicine and was taken to the vet. Paid: $500.

● An insured pet sitter was walking three dogs. One of the dogs spotted a cat sitting under a bush next to the sidewalk. The dog lunged and caught the cat's back leg. The cat was taken to the vet to be treated. Paid: $1,249.90.

● An insured pet sitter lost control of a dog, who then chased a cat. In the process, she scratched a car that was parked on the side of the street. Paid: $917.

● An insured pet sitter lost a client's key and had to call a locksmith that evening to come and let her in the house and change the client's locks. Paid: $197.

● An insured pet sitter was taking care of a client's two dogs. While in his care, they got into a fight. One dog was injured and was taken to the vet for treatment. Paid: $987.

These examples illustrate the necessity of carrying good business liability insurance and also the need for common sense and thorough thinking while on an assignment. Several of the claims might have been prevented if, for example, the pet sitter had bagged and disposed of the poop outside of the home rather than flushing it down the toilet; if the pet sitter had asked the Pug's owner for particular details about his breed and anything unusual he should be aware of while caring for the dog; or if the pet sitter had done her nails at her home instead of in her client's house!

Tip

During the initial interview, be sure to discuss with your client the nature of their pets' relationships. Find out whether they have a history of aggressiveness or fighting. It's a good idea to include this question on your service contract and make arrangements to keep the dogs separated, if necessary.

Please keep in mind that these examples have occurred over a ten-year span and that these are the "exception to the rule." It's kind of like flying: Millions of flights successfully and enjoyably take place each year. It's only the crashes or near misses that we hear about. Similarly, consider these unfortunate claims to be the "crashes" in pet sitting. Learn from them, so you don't end up being a "crash" victim!

HOW TO AVOID OR HANDLE OTHER PROBLEMS

Plain old problems come in all shapes and sizes. Problems that first come to mind about pet sitting are things like "What if I am bitten by a dog?" or "What if I lock myself out of a home?"

As I've mentioned before, you can avoid most of the problems associated with pet sitting by using common sense and by doing your homework beforehand. Your homework should include reading the following question-and-answer section, as well as the rest of this book. You should also research and seek out other sources that will help you intelligently and successfully operate your pet-sitting business. As with so many other things, an ounce of prevention is worth a pound of cure.

Q. *What if a pet I'm sitting for is hit by a car?*

A. First, protect yourself by having a clause in your service contract that releases you from that liability if a pet you are sitting for has free access to the outdoors. Cats may disappear for days and it's very possible they could be injured or killed, or they may simply never come home. If you're going to care for these free spirits, make sure you're protected with a signed release from liability. And while you're on the subject, point out to your clients the dangers of letting any pet roam free.

Second, many areas have leash laws that prohibit dogs from running free. Become familiar with leash laws and pet ordinances that apply to your community. As a reputable pet sitter, you would not want to risk violating such laws. Regardless of whether your area has a leash law, always walk a dog you're caring for on a leash. Point out to owners that they must provide a leash or allow you to supply your own. Otherwise, you will not be able to sit for their pets.

Third, ask the client during your first meeting if the pet is notorious for trying to dash out of a door when someone enters, or if the pet has ever gotten loose on his own. Knowing this history will help you prevent such problems. For pets who are prone to escaping out the door, try shaking a plastic market bag at the pet's height as you enter.

By taking these precautions, you will greatly minimize the chances that a pet will be hit by a car, or your liability if such an accident does occur.

Tip

In addition to the pet's identification tag, many pet sitters now have company identification tags they require each pet under their care to wear. The tags read, "I'm being cared for by XYZ Pet Sitters—999-8877" or, "If found, please contact XYZ Pet Sitters—999-8877." (You can see an example of this on page 93.) This is a great idea, because if a pet escapes and is found, the finder would try to call the pet's home phone (usually on the ID tag) and would not receive an answer because the owner is away. This simple but smart idea was suggested to me by a colleague. An investment for your business that will give you—and your customers—great peace of mind!

Q. How do I make sure a pet I'm sitting for doesn't run away or get lost?

A. Be sure to ask clients who have fenced areas for their pets if the enclosed area is secure. Often, dogs will have a favorite spot they dig at, trying to escape. You'll need to know where to look for this and how to remedy the situation. With the theft of pets an ongoing concern, you may want to require that all outdoor gates to pet areas be securely locked during the owner's absence. A locked gate will keep neighborhood children away from the pet, as well.

It's a smart idea to require that pets you sit for be current on all vaccinations and that they wear a collar with identification if they spend any time out of doors. You should also make notes on your service contract identifying the breed, sex, and age of the pet(s). This information may be helpful in identifying a pet or obtaining medical care, if necessary, while the owner is away.

Q. What if a repair person shows up at a client's home while I'm caring for a pet?

A. Never let anyone into a client's home unless you have been specifically authorized (in writing on your service contract) to do so by the client. Then do so only after the visitor has presented you with satisfactory identification. Even if it's the next-door neighbor wanting to borrow a cup of sugar or someone claiming to be a brother who always borrows the golf clubs, you can be held liable. Make it a strict company policy not to let anyone into a client's home other than emergency personnel (such as police, if necessary) and those mentioned in writing by your client.

Q. What if a client complains that I forgot to water the plants, as requested?

A. This is why your service contract is very important. Get all your instructions in writing. It is preferable, by the way, to let the client fill out the contract form. When the client has completed the form, review it carefully (making sure you can read the handwriting) and add any notations for yourself. By having the client complete the form, you ensure that your job responsibilities are clearly spelled out. If the plants aren't watered, it won't be because you forgot, but because the client failed to ask you to do so. A conscientious pet sitter will notice a room filled with plants and ask the homeowner if they need to be watered. If plants need this care, they will note this in the service contract.

As you may have noticed in the previous section, plant watering is among the top three reasons pet sitters have filed insurance claims. If you will be watering a client's plants, make sure no water is spilled on the furniture or hardwood floors, or any other place that may sustain water damage. Also make sure water faucets are completely turned off before leaving the premises.

Q. What if a toilet overflows when I try to flush the kitty litter?

A. Try to get specific instructions from the client about how to dispose of the litter. Never flush the litter unless your client has instructed you in writing to do so. If you are expected to dispose of it in the toilet, ask where the plumber's helper is stored in case there is a clogged drain. If a toilet does overflow, don't continue to use it. Instead, dispose of the litter in plastic bags to be placed in the outside garbage can.

It is a good idea to ask a client's permission before personally using a restroom in a home. Explain that sometimes it is necessary while working and ask if the client would mind (just as you would request permission if you were a guest in someone's home). If the client is agreeable, make sure that you leave the toilet as you found it (lid up or down) and that it is not still running when you leave the home.

Q. What if I'm late in getting to a client's home to feed and care for their pets?

A. This should not happen often, because your dependability is the basis of your reputation. However, if you find yourself delayed due to car problems, traffic jams, or mischievous critters at another customer's home, use your daily note to tell your client why you were late. Do your best to make sure your next visits are more prompt. Honesty is always the best policy. If you don't explain that you were late one morning, a watchful neighbor will probably inform your client of the fact, and you can expect a complaint.

Q. What if I notice a urine stain on the carpet?

A. Always ask your clients how pet accidents should be cleaned in their homes. Even if the client swears the pet is housetrained and accidents will not occur, get cleaning instructions just in case. Pets often behave differently when their owners are absent, and a change in toilet habits is typically how pets express their loneliness or boredom. If you live in an area where inclement weather sometimes precludes service rounds from being made safely, you can expect some puddles and messes that will need to be cleaned up.

Q. How do I handle a pet sitter on staff who tries to sell my clients other services that have nothing to do with my business?

A. As you increase your staff, you will probably find that many of your sitters have other jobs. It's important to instruct your sitters that while they are performing their pet-sitting duties, pet sitting should be their primary concern. Sitters should not approach customers for self-serving reasons while they are working for you. When a sitter goes to meet a pet owner, they should present your company's business card and talk pets—not real estate or homemade crafts. If the sitter acts more interested in recruiting a client's real estate business than the pet care at hand, the integrity of your service is diminished in the mind of the customer.

Q. What should I do about clients who return home earlier than anticipated but don't call to discontinue my services?

A. This lack of consideration causes pet sitters unnecessary trips, and I know of some sitters who have found themselves in embarrassing situations as a result. (One of my sitters arrived at the customer's home for a scheduled 6:45 a.m. visit, only to walk in on the client in his underwear making coffee in the kitchen! Needless to say, this was a startling and awkward situation for both parties. The client now calls immediately if he returns home sooner than expected.)

To protect and compensate yourself for these unnecessary trips, have a policy in writing, either in your company's brochure or the service contract, covering this situation. My inclination is to hit the client where it hurts (in the pocketbook) and charge full price for any wasted trips due to their negligence and lack of consideration. This is reasonable for your time, travel, and inconvenience, and may prompt the client to remember to call you when they return the next time.

Clients who do not notify pet sitters of their return, whether it's an early or expected arrival time, is a far too common complaint. To prevent this from becoming a problem in your business, emphasize to your client during the initial introductory meeting the need for notification upon return, and point out the monetary penalty (full charges for attempted visits) for failure to do so. A solution that has been well received is to leave a Client Reminder Card on your final visit, asking the customer to please call your office upon return. Consider having these printed on bright, eye-catching paper. (Similar cards are available for purchase; see the appendix for ordering information.)

Q. What do I say to clients who request late-night visits for their pets or who want additional services I don't generally perform?

A. As for the late-night visits, that is up to you. It is a company policy that needs to be determined in advance and strictly adhered to. Because the majority of my sitters were women and there was a greater risk of danger for them late at night, I did not offer late-night visits. I simply explained this policy to clients, and they always understood from a liability standpoint. I would much rather clean up pet messes the next morning than risk something happening to one of my staff members. There were only a couple of exceptions made to this rule. Both were instances where a pet required medication several times a day and the client was a long-standing customer. We made the visits but charged extra for doing so. Both clients were happy to pay the additional charge and realized that we were bending the rules to accommodate their special needs.

As for providing additional services, this, too, is something you'll need to consider in advance. If you're willing to comply with special requests, have either an hourly rate for your help or a per-task fee in mind. If time or liability constraints dictate that you stick strictly to pet-sitting chores, simply explain this to your client. This is why they called you in the first place, and they should understand that you aren't a jack-of-all-trades.

Q. What do I do if a client's teenager or college student appears unexpectedly at home and tells me that they will take over care of the pets?

A. Never take anyone's word for anything around the home except the person who hired you and signed the contract authorizing your services. This person is your employer and the one responsible for your bill. I've heard too many stories of teenagers or college students who are supposed to be at school or staying with someone. Instead, they sneak home to throw a big party while Mom and Dad are away. This scenario spells trouble. Tell the young person that you'll need to use the phone to call their parents and verify this fact, and speak with the client before ceasing any services.

Q. How do I prevent clients from calling their assigned sitter at home rather than making reservations through our office, as they should?

A. First, stress to all your sitters the importance of having all reservations made through your office. Point out how it could damage your company's reputation if a client calls only the sitter and leaves a message on an answering machine that services are needed immediately. What if the sitter is on vacation or is otherwise unavailable? The message would not be received, yet the client would leave assuming service would be provided. Because your office personnel should know which sitters are available and which are not at any given time, all reservations need to be made through the proper channel.

When a sitter understands this, they can tactfully explain the reason for your policy that clients must go through the office for reservations. If a client persists in calling the sitter directly, you'll need to call the customer yourself or write a letter that firmly requests cooperation in this matter. If a client still doesn't comply, then discontinue providing sitting services to this individual.

Some pet sitters have started including a phrase in the legal section of their service contract addressing this matter. The clause says something to the effect that "the client understands the necessity and agrees to make future reservations through the pet-sitting company. . . ." Because the service contract requires a client's signature, this becomes a written agreement.

Another reason you'll want all reservations coming through your office is if you provide liability insurance and a dishonesty bond. For this you'll need an accurate record of all sitting assignments undertaken by your company. If you have no documentation of the job, your insurance company may deny coverage on any claim related to it.

And speaking of insurance, it is vital. You *must* protect yourself. A pet may be lost or injured while under your care; personal property in a pet owner's home could be damaged or stolen; or other equally unsavory things might occur. One uninsured incident could ruin not only your business but your reputation as well. After clients hear that your insurance may not cover them unless reservations are made through your office, they're usually only too happy to request services this way.

Q. What if a client wants to make arrangements directly with the sitter in order to cut me out of the assignment?

A. It is a legitimate concern that clients and staff pet sitters could try to discretely work together and circumvent the company's involvement in an assignment. However, my experience has shown that this is not a big problem in the industry, for the following reasons:

● If you've done your homework and found good, honest people to work for your company, such dishonest activities will not take place.

● Entrepreneurship is not for everyone. Staff pet sitters, for the most part, are not out to steal your customers, especially if you've required that they sign a noncompete agreement before joining your company. Many people like having a supervisor or boss they report to and someone they can count on to support them.

● Pet sitters like the security of knowing they are protected by the company's insurance and dishonesty bond. This is valuable coverage to have and most pet sitters are happy to play by the rules in order to have the security it provides.

● Discuss these concerns with your attorney, who can advise you on steps you can take to keep your customers—and your business—yours.

Q. What immunizations should a pet sitter require of clients' pets?

A. Because I am not a veterinarian, I asked my veterinarian what she recommended for pets under my care. You should do the same. I made the suggestions my vet gave me a part of our company policies. The recommended immunizations included:

● Dogs: rabies, coronarvirus, parvovirus
● Cats: rabies, panleukopenia

Although my vet suggested that all vaccines are recommended for total protection, she said the preceding ones are the most important for pets receiving in-home care from a professional pet sitter.

When talking with your veterinarian, inquire about zoonotic diseases (illnesses humans can catch from pets). Some of these include ringworm, scabies, chlamydia, salmonella, cat scratch fever, Lyme disease, Rocky Mountain spotted fever, roundworms, and rabies. Find out how you can avoid transmission of these diseases and what their symptoms are. Check with your local health department about rabies vaccinations for you and your pet sitters. It's also a good idea for people who work with pets to remain up to date with tetanus vaccinations. And be aware that cat bites can be very serious. Because of the way cats lick and clean themselves, they have a lot of bacteria in their saliva. This bacteria can easily be transmitted to humans through a bite. If you or any staff members are bitten by a cat, it's wise to seek medical attention.

Q. My business has been open for six months and some days the phone doesn't ring. How long does it take to build a pet-sitting business and start making money?

A. That depends on several variables, such as location, perseverance, and advertising, which are discussed in detail in chapter 5. However, when someone calls or writes to ask me this question (someone who is usually having a down day), I always ask, "What have you done today to make your business a success? What did you do yesterday? What do you plan to do tomorrow?" Success does not just miraculously happen in any business—it takes work and determination. Although you have a great idea with a pet-sitting business and may be the smartest person in the world, you have to constantly work at selling your services. My advice is to try to do one thing each day that will help your business grow. Things you should try include:

- Distribute doorknob hangers in neighborhoods.
- Visit pet supply stores, groomers, or vet offices with business cards and something sweet for their morning or afternoon coffee break.
- Drop by doctor or dentist offices to see if you can leave some of your company newsletters as reading material in the waiting room.
- Call apartment complexes to see if they allow pets and, if so, if they would allow you to post a brochure or distribute doorknob hangers that advertise your services.

The list goes on and on. There are so many opportunities to educate, inform, advertise, and publicize your at-home pet care services. Seize every opportunity you can. Assertiveness is required to keep your phone ringing!

As for showing a profit and making money in this business, it was not until my third year of business that this began to happen for me. I've also heard from other pet sitters that the third year seems to be the magic one. However, with the wealth of information in this book and the numerous resources available to today's pet-sitting entrepreneur, I think an industrious and determined pet sitter can realize profits sooner.

Q. What about clients who want you to visit their cat every other day or who ask you to feed the dog but ignore the cat (and not charge) because they will leave plenty of food and water?

A. Daily visits are something else you'll be wise to discuss with your veterinarian. I think most veterinarians will recommend that pets be visited at least once a day—especially cats. Urinary blockages or other illnesses could be fatal for a cat who doesn't receive prompt medical attention. Besides, pets need love and personal attention, and it is this part of our service that makes pet sitting so popular. Determine what your visitation policy will be in advance. If you make any exceptions to the policy, make sure to note the circumstances in writing on your service contract.

For the client who asks that you ignore the cat, simply explain or put in writing on your company literature that your conscience would not allow you to overlook a cat in need of food, medical care, or human attention—so please don't request that the care of household felines be neglected!

THE BEST FROM THE BEST: TIPS FROM THE FIELD

As I mentioned earlier, I have learned so much from networking with other pet sitters through my many years in this business. Here are some tips I've picked up along the way that I'm sure will be helpful to you as a pet sitter. They are in no particular order; each is as important as the others.

- Carry an identification card in your wallet stating that you're a professional pet sitter. List on the card a person who should be contacted to take over pet-care visits if you are injured or ill.

- Ring the doorbell before entering homes, just in case the client has unexpectedly arrived home early.

- Pet owners should always be alerted to any problem you have, whether or not you think it's significant. Don't worry about bothering or disturbing them on a vacation—pets and homes are important to people!

- Never discuss clients and their travel plans over cell or cordless phones, because they might be monitored or overheard on other cordless phones or on scanner radio frequencies.

- Invest in a Polaroid or digital camera for your business. Take a photo of each pet for your files. A photo helps if a pet becomes lost and serves as documentation if there is any damage in the home.

- Don't place stacked mail where it can be viewed through a window. This is an indication that no one is home! If your client plans on checking their answering machine or voice mail while they're away, call and leave the client updates on how the pets are doing. Clients appreciate this caring touch! Bring any deliveries (newspapers, packages, water jugs, and so on) inside the home, or request a different delivery date.

- Use a lead pencil on any ornery keys—it makes them work like new! WD-40 also works well on temperamental house keys.

● Note any vehicles left in the client's driveway, such as make, model, license plate number, and color. This information will be useful during the owner's absence if there is a theft.

● Carry some jugs of water in your trunk. These may come in handy if you discover frozen pipes in a client's home.

● If it's too hot to take a dog for a walk and your client has a swimming pool, take the dog for a swim! Obtain permission from your client in writing before doing so.

● Keep a collapsible pet carrier and a pillowcase in your trunk. These things may be useful to transport a sick or injured animal.

● If a client's pet dies, send a pet sympathy card and/or make a contribution in the pet's name.

● Pill crushers are handy for pets requiring medication; however, always check with the pet's vet before crushing pills. Dispensing a crushed pill in a teaspoon of baby food (meat varieties) usually makes the task easier with cats and dogs. (Be sure to ask the vet if the pet has any food allergies.)

● Make your driving time productive. Keep a cell phone, books on tape, and a notebook and pen handy for use while driving or stuck in traffic jams.

● When testing a house key at the introductory interview, try to open the door after it has been closed and locked.

● Ignore possible temptations to use a client's swimming pool (unless previously authorized in writing!), exercise equipment, television, stereo, computer, and so on.

● Clip pet food coupons and leave them in the homes of clients who use that brand of food.

● For clients who have a burglar alarm, remember that the alarm company has a record of when the alarm is turned on and off. Some clients will use this record to ascertain the length of their pet-sitting visits!

● When talking to clients or leaving daily notes, use the pet's name frequently.

Chapter 8

Useful Business Forms

Professional, effective business forms are extremely important to any reputable pet-sitting service. A comprehensive form can save you valuable time, streamline your company procedures, protect your assets, and enhance your company's image. You'll be wise to devote your attention, energies, and money to developing forms that will best benefit your pet-sitting service.

In this chapter, I will give you an overview of the forms that are most highly recommended for a pet sitter and discuss some of their necessary components. Because a service contract will probably be your most important document, let's begin with that.

DESIGNING A SERVICE CONTRACT

You will use this form to gather information about each assignment. It will also serve as your legal agreement to perform pet-sitting services for a client on their premises. I highly recommend that you consult with a lawyer before using any contract you have written or purchased, to ensure that it adequately protects you. The following advice should help you prepare a rough draft or mock-up to review with your lawyer.

Client Information

The service contract can be divided into sections. The first section enables you to gather information about the client. You'll need spaces for the client's name, address, and home, cell, and business phone numbers. You'll want to know the date the customer is leaving town and when they anticipate returning. There should be room for the client to write where they can be reached (address and telephone number) while away.

You should also find out the name of a local friend, family member, or neighbor to contact in the event of an emergency, if you are unable to reach the client. After all, people on vacation do not sit in their rooms waiting for their pet sitter to call. If a home under your care is burglarized, the pet sitter probably won't know about valuables in the home that may be missing—something law enforcement officers need to know. Having a close friend or family member to call on may help in such a situation.

Other Keys

You should list on your service contract who else has a key to the home. This list can be part of the first section. There are several reasons why this is important. If the home is burglarized, the pet sitter will be able to provide the police with a list of key holders, which will aid in the investigation. Also, occasionally a client will have their home up for sale without displaying a FOR SALE sign. The sitter may arrive to care for a pet and find a real estate agent and a family of four walking through the home. Hopefully, reading this question on your service contract will remind the client to inform the sitter that a real estate agent has house keys. Finally, if a pet sitter does the unthinkable and gets locked out of the house, it's nice to know that the neighbor three doors away also has a key.

Natural Circumstances

If you live in an area that often has bad weather or natural disasters, you should have a formal disaster plan for your business. You should also have a written Plan B of action on your contract. Natural circumstances beyond your control may make it hazardous or impossible to make your pet-sitting visits. Having the name and number of a client's nearby neighbor may be a crucial part of Plan B.

Pet Information

The next portion of your contract should deal with the information you need to have about the pets. There are several things you'll want to include on your service contract: the pet's name, type, breed, sex, age, diet, medications, and exercise requirements. Leave enough room so you can make notations to yourself, such as "Taffy is the tabby cat and Samantha is the Siamese." It's important to have good notes; if you're sitting for several different clients on the same days, it can be easy to get instructions or pets confused.

Obtain the pet's medical history on your service contract. The little Chihuahua having seizures on your morning visit will throw you into a panic, unless you know this is normal for the dog and that rushing him to the vet isn't necessary. But if the seizures are not normal, you need to have the client's veterinarian's name and telephone number at hand. You should also obtain permission from the client to seek medical attention for their pet.

Something you may not think of asking is where the client stores the pet food. Not everyone keeps it in the same place. I've found it stored in pantries, garage trash cans, and bathroom closets; I've found it in containers on top of the refrigerator. Rarely is it stored in what you may consider to be a logical place. Save yourself time and a potential problem by learning this in advance.

You should know if the pet is allowed to have treats. Many owners are counting their pets' calories these days, and you don't want to sabotage any diets by offering treats.

Last but certainly not least, ask if the pet has any favorite forms of affection or exercise. If she loves to have her ears scratched or to chase a Frisbee, you want to know in order to make the most of the quality time you'll be spending with her. Find out what you can do to make the pet feel loved and happy during the owner's absence. It's this personalized part of your service that makes it so unique and appealing, and it's why the client most likely called you in the first place. Make sure you deliver lots of tender loving care.

Household Routines

The third section of your service contract should address pertinent information about the client's home. Spell out any additional household services you're willing to provide, and the extra fee for each chore. If you make a list, you or the client can simply check off what they would like done—the newspaper and mail brought inside, the lights alternated, the plants watered, and so on.

You might ask if the client wants the radio or television left on during their absence. This is a good crime deterrent because it creates noise and the impression of activity inside the home. It also provides companionship for some pets.

It's also a good idea to ask if the client wants you to answer their telephone when you're in the house. This was something I had not anticipated when I first began pet sitting. It was a strange feeling to be in someone's home and hear the phone ring and ring. I suppose it's almost a natural reflex or habit to want to answer a ringing phone! Shortly after this experience, there was an article in my local newspaper about a theft ring that had recently been caught in the act. The thieves had been calling homes and, if there was no answer, they would rob the home. Learning about this ingenious little scheme was all I needed to begin asking my customers if they wanted their telephones answered. Some customers feel it isn't necessary, while others appreciate the attention to detail this offer shows. When I am expected to answer the phone, I always act as if I am a full-time house sitter staying in the home. That way, if the caller is someone unscrupulous, this will hopefully prevent any wrongdoing. To date, though, it has always been a friendly voice on the other end of the telephone. Of course, I always leave the customer a message with the caller's name and number, as well as the date and time of the call.

With the popularity of answering machines today, a client may tell you just to let his or her machine take care of all calls. It's wise to ask the customer if they will be checking messages during their absence. If the answer is yes and you need to let the client know something that's not quite important enough for a long-distance call, you can leave a message on the answering machine. An example might be "This is Jane, your XYZ Pet Sitter. Just wanted to let you know that we had an unexpected snowfall last night with about eight inches of accumulation. Due to the record cold temperatures and snow, I brought your dogs into the basement to weather out the evening more comfortably. If there's any problem with leaving them inside during the evenings until it warms up some, please call me at home: (222) 999-2403. Thank you." Even if there's nothing newsworthy to report, it's still a nice idea to call and leave a message letting the client know everything is going well and that you hope they are having a good trip. If your client has an e-mail address and will be checking e-mail while they are away, you may want to communicate that way. A brief e-mail notifying them that everything is going well during their absence can be reassuring, and also speaks well for your professionalism.

Extra Services

Allow enough space in the third section of your service contract for notes about any extra services that may be requested. These will be tasks above and beyond your normal responsibilities. If you're willing to perform them, you will need to negotiate fees while meeting with the client, and write the fees down next to the description of the services. An example that comes to mind from my own experience is watering a client's greenhouse full of plants. My service fee normally allows for watering a few household plants, but this particular client, an avid horticulturist, was asking for more. Although I was happy to be able to help her by looking after the greenhouse, I did have to charge a considerable amount for the extra time. (I also had her sign a statement that said I would not be liable if any of her plants died—I truly do not have a green thumb!)

Another client wanted his dry cleaning picked up. One family, who was due to return late at night after a three-week trip to Europe, asked if some breakfast groceries could be left in their refrigerator. One of the funniest requests was to "feed the bread." Making sourdough bread requires keeping a starter base in the refrigerator and "feeding" it every few days with a couple of ingredients, such as potato flakes. This particular client said she felt like an idiot making the request but, needless to say, she was relieved and thrilled to learn I would do this for her while looking after her Poodles. It took only a minute or two to add the ingredients, so I didn't even charge her extra. At my first visit I found a freshly baked loaf of this wonderful bread left on her kitchen table as a gift for me. Sometimes it pays to be nice.

When discussing extras with clients, keep in mind that most people know if their requests are beyond the scope of your normal services. Usually they are more than happy to pay extra for special requests. So don't let a customer try to take advantage of you. Fortunately, not many will try to.

Returning House Keys

How you return a customer's house keys should be spelled out on your service contract. Returning a key personally may be the preferable way, because it gives you and the client peace of mind knowing the key got to its rightful owner. This visit also prompts the customer to pay you for your services at that time and often will get you a tip as well. However, returning house keys does take additional time and travel, so make sure your pet-sitting fees can absorb these costs, or consider charging a nominal amount for key return. As noted in an earlier chapter, many homes these days have deadbolt locks that require a key to lock them. Thus, these keys have to be returned personally.

Of course many clients will just adore your service and use it frequently. They will eventually request that you simply keep a key until further notice (see "'Always Ready' Service" in chapter 3). This is the ultimate compliment and my preferred procedure, but remember, keeping house keys increases your liability. Discuss this with your insurance agent and attorney, and be sure to safeguard clients' keys at all times.

Tip

Beware of the client (one without deadbolt locks) who instructs you to leave the key on the kitchen counter and lock yourself out of the home after your final visit. This would be fine, except that flights are missed or delayed, cars break down, and inclement weather may make it impossible for the owner to return when anticipated. If the key has been locked inside the home, an expensive locksmith will be necessary to enable you to continue caring for the pets. A word to the wise: Agree to leave the key well hidden outside for the client if they do not want it returned personally. This way, you still have access to the home, if necessary.

Fees and Hours

It's important to list your established fees and normal route hours on your service contract so that everything is clearly spelled out. However, some pet sitters prefer to have a separate fee schedule as an addendum to their business literature. The rationale is that if fees change, the whole service contract does not have to be reprinted. Regardless of the form you choose, make sure to include a place on your contract to fill in what the client's total fee will be. This should be understood and agreed upon before your services begin.

Also consider noting on your service contract whether any type of cancellation fee applies and under what circumstances. If something prevents a customer's trip from taking place, you still have to consider the time and travel pet sitters have invested in initial interviews, as well as the fact that your service was planning on this job as a source of revenue.

Another policy that may be important to list on your service contract is whether you have a one-time-only visit charge. An example of this would be the client who is going to a nearby town for a football game. He expects to return home later that same day and needs only one suppertime visit made to feed and exercise his dog. Unless your fee is a bit higher for these types of visits, they're probably not worth the time and effort of initial interviews and returning house keys.

Legal Considerations

The last part of a service contract should contain the clause(s) that explain exactly who is responsible for what regarding terms and conditions of the agreement. Making sure your service contract adequately protects you and makes your client feel comfortable is a delicate matter; it probably requires the advice and direction of an attorney. You want to be absolutely sure your service contract will be a binding agreement. When meeting with your attorney to draw up the contract, be sure to address the following questions:

- When and how must the customer pay for rendered services?

- Who is responsible for the veterinarian's fees if such assistance becomes necessary during the owner's absence?

- Who is responsible for extra time expended by a pet sitter due to emergencies regarding the pet or the home?

- Who is responsible for purchases—such as additional cat litter or paper towels—necessary for the satisfactory performance of duties?

- Under what circumstances, if any, can you or your company be held liable during the duration of the contract?

● Under what, if any, circumstances will the client be held liable during the duration of the contract?

● When do the terms of the contract actually begin and end?

● If other people will have access to the home at the same time you do, will the client release you from liability for any damage that could result from the other parties' negligence?

As you can see from the implications these questions bring to mind, having an inclusive service contract is extremely important. Although structuring this part of your contract may seem overwhelming, don't let it frighten you or prevent you from getting into the wonderful world of pet sitting. Just take your time, think through all these points, hash them out with objective friends or family members, and then visit a good attorney for advice and appropriate direction.

For those readers who don't relish the idea of designing a service contract, standard pet-sitting service contracts are available for purchase (see the appendix for ordering information). Whether you buy a service contract or create your own, consider a thorough and professional service contract to be a one-time investment that will guide you well in the years to come.

> ### Tip
>
> The legally binding aspects of a service contract are the signatures of the parties involved, so be sure your service contract has a signature line for the client and the pet sitter and a place for the date the contract was entered into. Make sure to obtain the client's signature on this critical document!

INVOICES

Some pet sitters give the client a copy of the service contract that lists the total amount due, and this serves as the customer's invoice. This procedure cuts down on accounting and postage costs. However, some clients don't realize that the service contract is their invoice, and they often have to be reminded of the payment procedure several times.

Other pet sitters have a separate invoice for billing. Some design this form themselves on a computer and have it preprinted with their company name, address, and logo; others purchase a basic invoice from an office supply store and personalize it with a rubber stamp.

Whichever method you choose, an invoice is a fairly basic and simple form. It usually includes an invoice number, a description of what the bill is for, and the date payment is due. Although not necessary, it's a nice gesture to include a self-addressed envelope with the invoice for the customer's convenience when paying.

Some pet sitters place postage on the self-addressed envelopes they leave for payment. I think this is an unnecessary gesture. After all, how many bills do you receive that include a stamped self-addressed envelope? Postage is expensive. However, the pet sitters who do this tell me they receive payment promptly, so the extra expense is worth it to them.

DAILY LOG

As I stated earlier, it's my opinion that every professional and reputable pet-sitting service needs some kind of daily log form. Some pet sitters simply use a scratch pad for writing the daily report for the client; others have professionally printed forms for these notes; still others use a checklist and mark off daily tasks as they are completed (notes can be made at the bottom of this form if the pet sitter observes anything of interest to the client).

Your own ideas and creativity may lead you to design a totally different type of daily log to meet the needs of your pet-sitting service, or you may prefer to purchase the camera-ready Daily Diary forms that are available (see the appendix for ordering information). In any event, I encourage you to make some kind of daily log an integral part of your service.

EVALUATION FORM

The value of this type of form to you as a business owner is immeasurable. It gives clients the chance to give you feedback that will keep your services on target and progressive. A well-designed evaluation form will help you assess what aspects of your services are well received and who is doing the best job delivering those services. After all, if you have a staff of pet sitters, they most likely work independently without direct supervision. You need some way of knowing about the job they are doing as representatives of your company. An evaluation form will provide this information.

Although some clients will not take the time to fill out and return an evaluation form, many of them will be impressed and complimented that their opinion matters and will eagerly respond. My clients were very helpful in returning this form and some made suggestions that improved our services.

I know of some pet sitters who leave a report card type of evaluation that lets the client grade the sitter's performance and note the customer's degree of satisfaction with services rendered. Others go into more detail, asking the client specific questions, such as "Did the pet sitter arrive in a timely manner?" "Was the pet sitter conscientious and caring?" and "Were your instructions followed?"

Another extremely important function of this form is that it enables you to ask clients how they first heard about your pet-sitting service. These replies can clue you in to what kind of advertising is bringing you results. And with the high cost of advertising, you do want to know where you're getting the most for your buck.

I insisted that my pet sitters leave a self-addressed evaluation form on their last visit to a customer's home. The recourse that this form offers our clients gives them a comfortable feeling about the professionalism of our service. If a client does not return an evaluation form, it's a good idea to follow up with a telephone call to make sure the client was pleased with your services.

CLIENT RESERVATION FORM

You'll use this form to schedule reservations and maintain basic information about each customer. It can be as simple as the Customer Card discussed in chapter 3, or you may want to expand it to an 8½-x-11-inch sheet or keep a more extensive client record on your computer.

The client reservation form needs to be easily accessible to you when taking phone reservations for services. It provides you with basic information at a glance, such as address, pet names, last dates of service, and assigned pet sitter. When you can speak more familiarly with a client, their comfort level increases—plus, they are impressed by your attention to detail!

Client reservation forms should include a space for special notations about a customer's needs (for example, "Mr. Smith's dogs love carrots as treats"). It also is helpful to include a column for customer payments and dates of payments. As discussed in chapter 3, this system can quickly tell you which accounts are delinquent.

NOTIFICATION FORMS

In recent years, pet sitters have found these forms to be extremely beneficial. There are three kinds of notification forms:

● **Vet Notification.** This form, or postcard, states that the customer's pet(s) will be under the care of your pet-sitting service for a certain time period. The client's signature on this form authorizes the veterinarian to administer medical care, as needed, during the owner's absence. This signed authorization also assures the vet that they will be paid by the customer (sometimes a monetary amount is specified) for medical attention. Vet offices usually make this form a permanent part of the customer's file.

● **Neighbor Notification.** This form, or postcard, notifies neighbors that personnel from your pet-sitting service will be caring for their neighbor's pet(s) during a specified time period. It should list a phone number where neighbors can reach you, if necessary. It's also helpful to list the car make and model the neighbor can expect to see visiting the home. With so much concern about crime and the popularity of neighborhood crime-stop programs, watchful neighbors will be glad to know that your service is authorized to be on their neighbor's premises. And you'll be glad that neighbors aren't calling law enforcement officials to investigate your presence in the neighborhood.

● **Police/Sheriff Notification.** This form, letter, or postcard informs the appropriate law enforcement agency that your service is authorized to visit the premises of the customer at the specified address during the specified time period. This notification alerts the agency that the client will be out of town (thus they may step up patrol of the area) and familiarizes them with your service. If you ever need to report a burglary or a problem at a client's home, it will be helpful if the law enforcement agency is aware of your business and reputation.

Notification forms also serve another important function. They advertise your service to the recipient. Neighbors may be more likely to call you for pet care when they know other people who use your services. Vets may be more likely to recommend your services after they see how many of their customers entrust their pet(s) to you. Law enforcement personnel may recommend you as a form of crime deterrence when they see how often the public relies upon your service for in-home pet care.

ADDITIONAL FORMS

The forms already discussed are probably the most basic for a professional pet sitter just starting out. However, as you discuss liabilities with your insurance agent and attorney, there may be strong arguments for developing other business forms.

For example, one sitting service I know has all clients fill out and sign a form that dictates their wishes in the event of their pet's death during the sitting assignment. Another has a separate form that pertains to the safekeeping and liabilities associated with the client's house keys. A third service has a more detailed form that deals with the health history and habits of each pet. A fourth uses an emergency repair form in case they encounter broken water pipes or another household emergency.

While some forms—such as a client information card, service contract, and brochure—are found in all pet-sitting businesses, others are developed to meet the personal needs of each service.

Of course, as your business grows you'll need things such as employment application forms. Standard employment applications can be purchased in most office supply stores, but they are rudimentary in nature. With the unique demands of pet sitting, a more comprehensive employment application form is required to help you determine which candidates are best suited for your openings. With time, you'll soon know the questions to ask job applicants and will be able to design your own application or alter a store-bought form accordingly. To avoid violating any state or federal hiring laws, it's advisable to consult with an attorney about any employment application you use in your business.

TIPS FROM PET SITTERS

Tips about business forms from other pet sitters include the following:

● Be sure to ask on your service contract if the pet knows any commands. This information can come in handy when you're trying to get a dog to sit or stop jumping on you!

● Ask clients for the dates of their pets' birthdays, then surprise them with a pet birthday card or gift. Clients will love your thoughtfulness!

● If your clients are flying while traveling, find out the airline and flight number and write it on your service contract. Although airline crashes are rare, it's useful information to have on hand if one occurs or if you simply want to make sure that a client's return flight is arriving on time.

● For a humorous and personal touch, set aside a section on the front of your business envelopes where you can write a personalized note or greeting to the household pet.

Chapter 9

Buying, Selling, or Closing a Business

With proper planning, it is possible to have a long and rewarding career in professional pet sitting. However, sometimes circumstances (family needs, job transfers, retirement, burnout) require you to get out of the business. When it's time to say good-bye to this career, you most likely will have two options: closing your business or selling it. I hope the investment you have made in starting and growing your pet-sitting service will be something you can sell to realize a nice financial return. If you're making money as a pet sitter, you don't want to just close the doors and quit. The business you have built may be worth more than you think.

Although selling or leaving the business may be the last thing on your mind as you ponder getting into pet sitting, I have included the subject in this book because the industry has evolved to the point that the sale of pet-sitting businesses is becoming commonplace.

Keep in mind that selling a service business is a little different than selling a retail outlet or product-oriented venture. With the latter, you most likely have inventory, a building or a lease for business space, fixtures, and equipment, as well as a business name, reputation, and goodwill. In a service business such as pet sitting, there are more intangible assets. You probably have a trademarked name, established operating procedures and forms, a client list, and your reputation and goodwill. Although reputation and goodwill are extremely important assets, their value is often harder to establish than the value of a building or retail inventory.

If you've intentionally kept your pet-sitting service small and worked out of your home, you most likely have only your client list to sell. With the growth of the pet-sitting industry, this is becoming a more frequent occurrence. What typically happens is that another area pet sitter or pet-sitting firm buys the client list for either a set amount per name or a percentage of business revenues realized from the customer over the next year or other set period. In the percentage method, the purchasing pet sitter usually makes a down payment and then makes the final payment at the end of the specified term. The selling pet sitter usually notifies customers in writing about the sale of the client list, recommends the new pet-sitting service, and thanks the clients for their past business. Some closing pet sitters even take the purchasing pet sitter around to personally introduce them to clients and their pets. Although an outright purchase of a client list (so much per name) results in a faster up-front payment, the percentage procedure can eventually result in a higher price for the seller. Discuss these options with your accountant and attorney.

> **Tip**
>
> Whether you're buying or selling a pet-sitting business, be sure to seek advice from your accountant and attorney.

If you have built a thriving and lucrative pet-sitting business, talk with your accountant before starting the sales process. See if they can help you set a value on your business and discuss the tax ramifications of selling for a lump sum versus on installment. Determine in advance if you can afford to finance any of the selling price. There could be a person well suited to your business who is interested but who doesn't have all the cash readily available. (I know of some staff pet sitters who have bought businesses from the owners when the opportunities presented themselves. The owners were confident in selling to them and financing part of the sale because they knew the work ethic of these employees.)

HOW A BUSINESS BROKER CAN HELP

When you're thinking of selling, it's a good idea to talk with a business broker. Ask your accountant for a recommendation or check your local Yellow Pages for listings. Business brokers sell businesses every day and they may have someone in mind who would be a strong candidate to buy your business. A business broker can also help you determine an asking price or confirm the figure you and your accountant have come up with. Additional benefits of using a business broker are the convenience and confidentiality these professionals provide. A business broker can run a blind ad, screen potential candidates, and arrange for personal meetings with you only when a candidate seems like a good prospect. Find out at the outset what the business broker's fees are and try to find one who charges only when a sale goes through.

A business broker can advise you about what financial information you'll need to provide. This will include past tax returns, profit-and-loss statements, equipment and asset lists, and lease agreements. If a buyer wants to make an offer for your business, the broker, as an objective third party, can keep personalities from damaging a prospective sale. Once a price and terms are agreed upon, the broker can prepare a buy-and-sell agreement; then attorneys and accountants will become involved to work out the final details. If you decide to list your business with a business broker, be prepared to give them an exclusive right-to-sell contract for at least six months. Buying a business is a major decision; it usually takes time to find the right buyer.

Selling my pet-sitting business was an emotion-packed experience. Although my mind knew it was the right thing to do, my heart was having second thoughts. I had poured so much of myself into building the business that it was, in many respects, like my child. Could I really let go? Yet, when the attorney handed me my check at the closing, the feeling was exhilarating—realizing the fruits of your labor is very rewarding!

Keep in mind while contemplating your pet-sitting business, and while running and building it, that the decisions and actions you make and take will affect the final disposition of your business. Whether you leave the business to your children or sell it, you want to have built something of value that has brought you pleasure and pride.

THE P'S AND Q'S OF SAYING GOOD-BYE

Just as there are steps to take when starting a pet-sitting business, there is protocol to follow when closing or leaving your business. Remember how excited you were about starting your pet-sitting service and how you wanted to do everything the right way so you would be a success—and a credit—to the industry. Let that same philosophy guide you as you leave the profession. Steps to take include:

● Notify your customers of your decision to sell or close the business. Inform them of their future options for in-home pet care. Specify how the return of house keys will be handled.

● When returning client house keys, have each customer sign an acknowledgment that their keys have been returned.

● Notify your business insurance and bond provider of the change in ownership or closing of the business.

• Notify any professional affiliations, such as Pet Sitters International or your local chamber of commerce, of the change in ownership or closing of the business. Otherwise, you may still continue to receive referrals from the Pet Sitters International Locator Line. This could be annoying as well as embarrassing to the organization giving out incorrect information.

• Offer to provide letters of recommendation for staff members who may be losing their positions due to the closing or sale of the business.

• Talk with your accountant and attorney to make sure the proper documentation has been filed with your city or state regarding the sale of your business or the closing of your corporation.

THINKING OF BUYING?

Opening a pet-sitting business is not that difficult, nor is it that expensive compared to some business opportunities. The question becomes, in essence, do you want to build the car yourself or do you want to jump in and just drive?

You may prefer to investigate the possibility of buying an existing pet-sitting business rather than starting your own. Sometimes it can be more economical to purchase a business instead of starting from scratch. A good place to look for businesses that are for sale is in *The WORLD of Professional Pet Sitting*, the bimonthly magazine published by PSI.

Are there advantages in purchasing a ready-made business over and above what you could do by yourself, or want to do by yourself? If you do not see any benefit to building your own business, then buying a pet-sitting service is an option to pursue.

The primary advantage to buying an established pet-sitting business is that the set-up work has usually been done for you and a client base, along with a good reputation, already exists. Often a seller

> ### *Tip*
>
> If you're thinking of selling or buying a business, the publication *Selling Your Pet Sitting Business*, written by my respected colleague Bill Foster (see the appendix for ordering information), provides helpful information for sellers and buyers.

is willing to provide some hands-on training to the new owner and ensure a smooth transition between the new owner, staff members, and clientele. If the business is currently making a profit, a new owner just has to keep steering the business in the same direction or take it to new heights.

Chapter 10

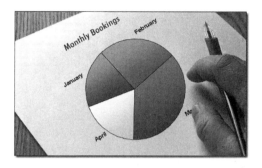

Tracking Trends

You will find it helpful to chart such data as the number of inquiries you receive each day about your service and the actual number of bookings or assignments per month, per holiday, per zip code, and so on. You can chart this information by making check marks on a calendar or map, or by keeping a log of customer names by various categories. Of course, today's computer software can simplify these statistical tasks!

It's important to review these records regularly to help you plan and set goals for your business. Plus, you will have a discouraging day every now and then, and referring to these statistics to see how you've grown since last Easter or Labor Day is reassuring.

Keeping these types of records also helps you learn the busiest areas and times for your business. Knowing this information will assist you in staffing appropriately and scheduling the best time for your own vacations.

ANALYZING YOUR BUSINESS TRENDS

My business grew to the point that it was steady year-round, and that's what most members of PSI report today with their businesses. Sometimes there will be slower periods, such as the couple of weeks when kids go back to school, the first couple of weeks in November before the holiday season begins, and usually for a short period right after the new year.

I found that my busiest season began with Easter and continued through Labor Day. This is the traditional family vacation period and has the nicest weather. September and October were also good months for us because many clients went on fall fishing trips and foliage tours, and some preferred to vacation when the kids were back in school. November brought lots of Thanksgiving reservations, and Christmas was the busiest holiday of all.

The slower months were January, February, and March, probably due to people rebounding from holiday spending, computing their taxes, or just plain nesting in bad weather. I always used the slower months to recuperate from the busy season, clean out my files, and catch up on paperwork. I also tried to get away to some warm, sunny destination.

Today's pet sitters tell me that the winter months are busy for them now with business from skiers, snowbirds, and families who vacation during school breaks and winter holidays. This makes perfect sense, because people travel for many reasons: business, pleasure, and often because of family emergencies. Some people prefer a January vacation, while others always vacation the third week of July. There is no rule for when people travel. The upside to this is that you'll find your pet-sitting services are needed throughout the year. The downside is that there's no sure way to predict the amount of business you'll do each month, and this can be frustrating.

Tip

Midday dog walking has become the bread and butter of many pet-sitting services in large metropolitan areas. Advertising your services as useful for in-town pet owners as well as those who must travel is a great idea. Doing so may increase your volume of business.

Don't be surprised to find your services in demand even when a client is not leaving home. Sometimes pet owners need help due to an illness or injury that prevents them from properly caring for their pets. I recall several new mothers, overwhelmed with the demands of an infant, who called to request pet-care services. They couldn't juggle new-baby needs with necessary dog walks and pet care. Other times, long working hours may prompt a pet owner to request your services. And some dog owners, kept busy at work, will want a monthly contract with you to walk and exercise their pooches at lunchtime each day.

CRIME DETERRENCE

Another business trend has occurred due to the level of crime in today's society. Many pet sitters market the added benefit of crime deterrence that in-home visits provide; this trend has resulted in requests for house checks from people who don't even own a pet. These clients simply like the crime-deterrent services of newspaper and mail pickup, plant watering, and rotating which lights are on. You may want to emphasize this aspect of your pet-sitting services in your advertising.

Unless you are licensed as a security or law enforcement officer, however, don't advertise crime-deterrent activities as providing "security" services. This can be a liability issue if a home is burglarized and you've promoted yourself as a security service. Remember, your first and foremost responsibility is to provide pet care in the client's home. As a courtesy you simply try to give a home a "lived-in" look as a crime deterrence measure.

OVERNIGHT PET AND HOUSE SITTING

Another growing trend is that of overnight pet-sitting services. Some clients whose pets are used to sharing their owner's bed prefer that someone actually stay overnight in their home to provide this additional companionship for their beloved pets. Others like the additional crime deterrence provided by someone living in the home. Additional time, liabilities, and rules are involved when a pet-sitting service provides sleepover services. Give careful thought to adding such services. The following questions are just some of the issues to consider:

- What hours will the pet sitter be required to stay in the home?

- Will the customer or the pet sitter provide food for meals?

- What is the pet sitter allowed to use in the home (for example, the television, microwave, stereo, and so on)?

- Can the pet sitter entertain guests while living in a customer's home?

As you can see by these questions, overnight pet sitting involves a different set of variables. More than likely, you'll need a separate service contract for overnight pet-sitting or house-sitting assignments. However, there is lots of potential business out there for a pet-sitting service that employs reliable, caring, and trustworthy sitters who are bonded, insured, and security-checked to provide overnight care.

EXPANDED SERVICES

One other trend our industry is experiencing is that of add-on services. These include working with mobile groomers to provide in-home grooming services, delivering premium pet foods to busy clients, and, as mentioned earlier, pet transportation services to vet appointments or groomers for working pet owners. The positive reception to these additional services is further proof of the love affair we have with our pets!

CLOSING THOUGHTS

Every successful endeavor begins with one small step. By purchasing and reading this book, you've taken that first step toward opening your own successful business.

Pet sitting has provided me with an enjoyable, challenging, and rewarding career. As I have mentioned, little information was available to guide me when I began pet sitting. I had to work long and hard to develop a successful business and elevate pet sitting to a recognized, respectable, and credible livelihood. Now that pet sitting has become an established industry, the demand for at-home pet care is only going to grow as pet owners learn of its advantages and conveniences. Tremendous potential exists for pet sitters who are willing to work hard to operate a reputable and professional pet-sitting service.

Now it's up to you. Pet sitting is an exciting, interesting, and fun business that requires a relatively low up-front investment. The need for this service exists in large and small communities—and you can meet it with your sincere and energetic commitment to provide the best in personalized home pet care. Remember that the pioneers in this field are counting on you to uphold and continue the standards of excellence that are necessary for successful pet sitters. I hope this book will make meeting this requirement much easier for future pet sitters everywhere.

Appendix

ESTIMATED START-UP COSTS CHECKLIST

Business License(s) _____

Name Registration _____

    Local _____

    State _____

    Federal _____

Attorney Fees

    Business Name Consultation and Registration _____

    Legal Structure Costs (partnership agreement, _____
        incorporation, and so on)

    Business Form Development and Review _____

Accountant Fees _____

Liability Insurance _____

Dishonesty Bond _____

Disability Income Insurance _____

Deposit for Office Space _____

Automobile Umbrella Coverage _____

Rent for Office Space _____

Moving Expenses for Office Site Setup _____

Bank Charges _____

Business Telephone Deposit _____

Business Telephone Installation _____

Monthly Charge for Business Telephone _____

Telephone (Purchase or Rental) _____

Answering Machine and/or Personal Answering Service _____

Cell Phone and/or Pager _____

Monthly Cell Phone Calling Plan   _____
Monthly Internet Connection Fee   _____
Calculator   _____
Computer   _____
Software Program(s)   _____
Desk   _____
Chair   _____
File Cabinet   _____
Shelf or Bookcase   _____
Business Form Design   _____
Business Form Printing   _____
Business Form Purchase   _____
Basic Office Supplies   _____
Pet-Sitting Supplies   _____
Office Library Books and Videos   _____
Advertising
    Web Site Design   _____
    Monthly Hosting   _____
    Newspaper   _____
    Yellow Pages   _____
    Radio   _____
    Television   _____
    Local Publications   _____
    Other   _____
Annual Dues for Professional Affiliations
and Subscriptions
    Pet Sitters International   _____
    Chamber of Commerce   _____
    Pet-Related Organizations   _____
    Better Business Bureau   _____
Reference Books
    Business-Related   _____
    Pet-Related   _____
    Other   _____
Magazine Subscriptions
    Business-Related   _____
    Pet-Related   _____
    Other   _____
Convention Registration and Travel   _____
Miscellaneous   _____
    Total   _____

HELPFUL PRODUCTS FOR PROFESSIONAL PET SITTERS

As I stated at the outset, much of what I initially learned about the pet-sitting business was through trial and error. My goal in writing this book has been to save other prospective pet sitters some of the hassle, headaches, and expense I went through in establishing and successfully operating my own business. In my many years in this field, I've found some ideas, methods, and products to be extremely beneficial. So other pet sitters do not have to "reinvent the wheel" and to improve the standards of the pet-sitting industry, I've made many of these useful and favored items available through my pet-sitting supply company, Patti Moran's. A partial list of some of these products follows. They're all tried-and-true products that will assist you in operating your pet-sitting business efficiently, economically, and professionally. A catalog and my web site (www.pattimoran.com) describe these and other products in more detail. Be sure to mention that you're a reader of this book, because the catalog is free to readers!

● **Professional Pet-Sitting Starter Kit.** Enables you to start pet sitting professionally easily and economically. Available in three versions to meet your career goals.

● **Videos.** *Professional Pet Sitting—The Basics* and *Professional Pet Sitting Tips from the Pros* are informative videos on professional pet sitting. They can be valuable training aids for all pet sitters.

● **Business Forms for Pet-Sitting Professionals.** These forms save you valuable time and streamline your office procedures while enhancing your company's image. Everything from the all-important service contract and sitter evaluations to employment applications is available. Each camera-ready form may be reprinted by your local printer.

● **PZZZ . . . Ads Advertisement Campaign.** A successful, market-tested ad campaign that brings your service increased revenues and name recognition while bringing a smile to your customers' faces. Seasonal, holiday, and year-round ads are available. Camera-ready material.

● **Professional Pet Sitter Apparel.** T-shirts, sweatshirts, sweatpants, and shorts. Comfortable and colorful, this line of casual attire enables you to look neat, promote your profession, and be prepared for muddy paws.

And there's more! Pet first-aid kits and books . . . doorknob hangers . . . pet placemats . . . client reminder cards . . . daily diaries . . . a business plan for pet sitters . . . *Selling Your Pet Sitting Business* by Bill Foster . . . survival bags and pet-sitting "paks" . . . brochure stands . . . and more! For more information about these and other products, please write or call:

Patti Moran's
418 East King St.
King, NC 27021
Orders only: (800) 380-PETS
Fax (orders only): (336) 983-3755
Customer service: (336) 983-2444
E-mail: info@pattimoran.com
www.pattimoran.com

PET AND BUSINESS-RELATED ORGANIZATIONS

The following list contains contact information about organizations that may be of interest to pet-sitting entrepreneurs.

Pet Information

American Animal Hospital Association (AAHA)
12575 West Bayaud Ave.
Lakewood, CO 80228
(303) 986-2800
www.aahanet.org

American Humane Society
63 Inverness Drive East
Englewood, CO 80112
(800) 227-4645
Fax: (303) 792-5333
www.americanhumane.org

American Pet Products Manufacturer's Association (APPMA)
255 Glenville Rd.
Greenwich, CT 06831
(203) 532-0000
Fax: (203) 532-0551
www.appma.org

The American Society for the Prevention of Cruelty to Animals (ASPCA)
424 E. 92nd St.
New York, NY 10128-6804
(212) 876-7700
www.aspca.org

The Humane Society of the United States
2100 L Street, NW
Washington, D.C. 20037
(202) 452-1100
Fax: (301) 258-3074
www.hsus.org

Disaster Planning Information

United Animal Nations Emergency Animal Rescue Services (EARS)
P.O. Box 188890
Sacramento, CA 95818
(916) 429-2457
Fax: (916) 429-2456
www.uan.org/ears/

Noah's Wish
P.O. Box 997
Placerville, CA 95667
(530) 622-9313
Fax: (530) 622-9313
www.noahswish.org

Information for Small Business Owners

National Foundation of Independent Business
Administrative Office
53 Century Blvd, Suite 250
Nashville, TN 37221
(800) NFIB-NOW (634-2669)
www.nfib.com

National Foundation for Women Business Owners
Center for Women's Business Research
1411 K Street, NW, Suite 1350
Washington, DC 20005-3407
(202) 638-3060
Fax: (202) 638-3064
www.nfwbo.org
www.Womensbusinessresearch.org

Pet Sitters International
201 East King St.
King, NC 27021
(336) 983-9222
Fax: (336) 983-5266
www.petsit.com

PSI RECOMMENDATIONS FOR EXCELLENCE IN PET SITTING

Recommended Quality Standards for Excellence in Pet Sitting

- The sitter is bonded and insured.

- The sitter provides references.

- The sitter has adequate knowledge and experience caring for pets and is clearly mindful of their safety and well-being.

- The sitter provides written literature describing services and stating fees.

- The sitter visits the client's home before the first pet-sitting assignment to meet the pets and get detailed information about their care.

- The sitter shows a positive attitude during the initial meeting and seems comfortable and competent in dealing with animals.

- The sitter wants to learn as much as possible about the animals in his or her care.

- The sitter provides a service contract that specifies services and fees.

- The sitter is courteous, interested, and well informed.

● The sitter keeps regular office hours and answers client inquiries and complaints promptly.

● The sitter takes precautions to make sure a client's absence from home is not detected because of any careless actions or disclosures by the sitter.

● The sitter conducts business with honesty and integrity and observes all federal, state, and local laws pertaining to business operations and animal care.

● The sitter has a veterinarian on call for emergency services.

● The sitter has a contingency plan for pet care in case of inclement weather or personal illness.

● The sitting service provides initial and ongoing training for its sitters.

● The sitting service carefully screens applicants for employment.

● The sitter calls to confirm or has the client call to confirm that the client has returned home as scheduled.

● The sitter refrains from criticizing competitors.

● The sitter provides a service rating form for clients.

● The sitter exhibits courtesy and professionalism in all dealings with staff members, customers, and industry colleagues to present the pet sitter and the pet-sitting industry favorably and positively.

POSTSCRIPT

As I've said, the wealth of information contained in this book is a compilation of my own personal learning experiences in pet sitting as well as many tips shared with me by colleagues through the years. I truly believe that this sharing of information and desire to see each other succeed is something unique and special within our industry. So if you learned from anything in this book, please repay the favor as you learn and grow in professional pet sitting. Please write or e-mail me at patti@petsit.com about things you find helpful and successful in your pet-sitting service. I'll try to incorporate them in future editions.

It's a big world out there with lots of room for successful pet-sitting services. Let's help ourselves, our colleagues, and our industry be the best we can be. I wish you good luck and good fortune with your pet-sitting business!

Index

About the Author

Patti J. Moran developed pet sitting as a profession after starting her own pet-sitting business, Crazy 'Bout Critters, in Winston-Salem, North Carolina, in 1983. One of the first to enter the industry, Moran learned as her business grew, always stressing quality and professionalism in the delivery of pet-sitting services. After word of her business spread to other parts of the United States, Moran was prompted to put her how-to advice on paper and first published *Pet Sitting for Profit* in 1987. Shortly after that, requests for her pet-sitting business forms led to the start of her products company, Patti Moran's Products for Professional Pet Sitters.

As others joined her in the profession, Moran began the National Association of Pet Sitters in 1989 and also founded Pet Sitters International in 1994. With more than 7,500 members in the United States, Canada, and other nations, PSI is the largest association of professional pet sitters in the world.

Moran is a graduate of the University of North Carolina at Chapel Hill. She and her husband, Mike, are allowed to live in their home with five spoiled canines and two felines.